# WOODEN BOAT BUILDING

## HOW TO BUILD A DRAGON CLASS SAILBOAT

**Nick Loenen**

Published by:

## FriesenPress

Suite 300 – 852 Fort Street
Victoria, BC, Canada V8W 1H8

www.friesenpress.com

Distributed to the trade by The Ingram Book Company

# Index

List of Figures . . . . . . . . . . . . . . . . . . . . . . . . . . . . . . . . v

Acknowledgements . . . . . . . . . . . . . . . . . . . . . . . . . . . ix

Foreword . . . . . . . . . . . . . . . . . . . . . . . . . . . . . . . . . . . xi

*Introduction*
**Peak Moments** . . . . . . . . . . . . . . . . . . . . . . . . . . . . . . . 1

*Chapter One*
**Planning, Design, Costs, Skills** . . . . . . . . . . . . . . . . . . 7

*Chapter Two*
**Shop, Sharpening, Steam box** . . . . . . . . . . . . . . . . . . 17

*Chapter Three*
**Lofting, Steam Bending, Laminating Frames** . . . . . . . . . 47

*Chapter Four*
**Frames and Hull.** . . . . . . . . . . . . . . . . . . . . . . . . . . . . . . 65

*Chapter Five*
**Planking, Colour Scheme, Turning Hull, Lead Keel** . . . . . 85

*Chapter Six*
**Coaming, Deck, Engine, Cuddy, Seats, and Sole** . . . . . . . . 111

*Chapter Seven*
**Mast, Boom, Blocks and Bright Work.** . . . . . . . . . . . . . . . 133

*Chapter Eight*
**Weighing Anchor and Sailing Tips** . . . . . . . . . . . . . . . . . 153

**Appendix (Saw Filing)**............................... 169

**Glossary**........................................... 177

# List of Figures

| # | Name | Page # |
|---|------|--------|
| #1 | Retractable Brackets for Holding Stock | 22 |
| #2 | Scissor Truss | 20 |
| #3 | Raising a Power Pole | 25 |
| #5 | Oil Stone portable Platform with Honing Guide | 30 |
| #6 | Old fashioned Saw Sharpening Horse for Filing Hand Saws | 171 |
| #7 | Steam Box Fired by Electric Kettle | 33 |
| #8 | Bending Jigs | 35 |
| #9 | Wooden Wood Lathe with Sanding Disk | 38 |
| #10 | Roller on Adjustable Stand | 40 |
| #12 | Simple Bending Jig | 58 |
| #13 | Reverse Curve Bending Jig | 61 |
| #14 | Construction Frame | 66 |
| #15 a&b | Pulpit | 78-79 |
| #16 | Knife-sharp Bow Stem | 93 |
| #17 | 'Shoe' for Rudder Shaft | 98 |
| #18 | Half Wheel for Turning Hull | 106 |

#19     Control Panel and Cockpit: Typical Cross Section     113

#20     Aft of Cockpit Cross Section     124

#21     Mast Cross Section     134

#22     Top of Mast Assembly     138

#23     Wood Block     145

For the upcoming generation and dedicated to
*Anthony, Erica, Andrew*
*Seth, Rebecca, Asher*
*Shaelyn, Nicolas, Alexandre*
*Tristan, Dominic, Jordan*

may your future include
wind, water, waves, wood
building boats, boating
sails, sheets, and sailing!

# ACKNOWLEDGEMENTS

Building a boat and writing about it are mostly solitary pursuits. But humans cannot function apart from past history and present community. Neither the building project nor this book would exist without the contribution of many, past and present.

During the more than six years of construction and several years prior I consulted widely. Yet, errors were made which could have been avoided had I tried a little harder to involve others. To all who gave advice I am grateful, in particular the following.

Aedgard Koekebakker dropped in twice for several days while on a solo sailing trip to Alaska. We discussed every aspect of constructing *Lady Jayne* from stem to stern, above deck and below deck. Aedgard is knowledgeable and passionate. He was project manager for Connie van Rietschoten's *Flyer II,* winner of the 1981-82 Whitbread Round the World Race. In his day van Rietschoten was the best yachtsman in the world in the Dragon class. I benefitted greatly from Aedgard's interest and enthusiasm.

Bob Fielding gave wise advice about the exhaust system and through-hull fitting suitable for an air-cooled engine in a wooden boat, how best to link the engine to the propeller shaft and designing bolts for anchoring the lead keel to the hull. Long-time friend Hank Roos, who helped make the launch of my first sailboat such a memorable event, gave advice and assisted rolling the hull. Bradley and Stephanie Garner were always helpful particularly regarding the challenges of launching a deep-keel boat on a ramp from a trailer. Ed Loenen's artistic talent shines in the pleasing colour scheme and Cor de Bruin's expertise as master painter shaped the preparation and application of paint and varnish. Rick McBride helped design rigging and sails.

Arie de Kleer, friend and life-long professional boat builder was most helpful of all. His generous gift of time and expertise stretching over many years were invaluable and are deeply appreciated.

Friend, Hans Bomhof drafted professional sketches to convey the meaning of the text better than words. Jeff Loenen uncovered grammatical embarrassments and awkward sentences. Heather Loenen is credited with the photos except for pages (164 and 168) which were taken by Heidi Sicka and Mejan Reijm, respectively. Louise Todhunter and Michael Loenen gave advice on marketing in an on-line world.

My life partner, wife Jayne has always encouraged me in whatever path I followed. To her and all who supported me I am indebted and express my gratitude. Errors that remain are mine alone.

Lee Bay, Pender Harbour, BC
November, 2011

# FOREWORD

My wife Ann and I retired to Garden Bay in Vancouver's Expo year (1986) after selling my business and having our 5 children grow up and leave the nest. We were lucky enough to have a comfortable sailboat and purchased a waterfront lot with a dock that put us right in the middle of the water activities of the village of Pender Harbour.

Interest in sailing small boats arose in my university years (1949–1954) when I was crew on a two-person Star class sailboat that raced in Vancouver's English Bay as well as various regattas from Vancouver Island to Puget Sound. Now in my ninth decade, I still enter year round the weekly harbour race organized by the *Garden Bay Sailing Club*. I confess to a life-long love for sailboats and the sea. Sailing is healthy, stimulating and endlessly challenging.

After moving it was not long before we fell in love with the Pender Harbour area of the Sunshine Coast renowned for its sun, wind, waves, water and enchanted coastline. The Sunshine Coast is located just North-West of Vancouver between two fjord-like inlets - Howe Sound and Jervis Inlet. Its idyllic setting has always attracted artists, artisans and those with creative talents who quietly make a wonderful contribution, enriching the lives of all.

The Dragon shows speed even when becalmed

In particular, from the earliest days its people have had a special bond with boats and water. How can it be otherwise, the Sunshine Coast is inaccessible, except by water! Its earliest residents, the Coast Salish Sechelt Nation built and paddled ornately decorated cedar dugout canoes to their summer fishing villages. The European settlers were sustained by fishing and logging for many generations, requiring boats of all descriptions. Today, this unique coast is a recreational boaters' paradise.

Soon after our arrival I met many like minded individuals. Zoro Szabados, for example, whose well-appointed workshop has turned out a small fleet of wooden sailboats including his latest project, a thirty-foot Herreshof which is nearing completion. Zoro does this while sailing the harbour at every opportunity.

From these early contacts, eventually the *Garden Bay Sailing Club* materialized. The club rejuvenated the Malaspina Annual Regatta and introduced harbour races every Saturday, year round. Both races are open to sail keelboats of all classes, entered by members, local residents, and visitors alike. For information visit: www.gardenbaysailingclub.com

Nick Loenen followed Zoro's lead. *Lady Jayne* was built at Lee Bay, between the mouth of the harbour and Agamemnon Channel. Launched in the summer of 2006, she entered her first harbour race on Saturday, June 21, 2007 and has been a regular entry during the summers since. *Lady Jayne* was on show at the Sunshine Coast Wooden Boat Show in Madeira Park, 2008, receiving the coveted Judges Award for best overall and went on to win her division at the 20th Malaspina Annual Regatta, 2009, plus the Race Committee Award the same year.

To me, the strikingly sleek lines of the *Lady Jayne*, a Dragon class keel boat, have the remarkable ability to make it look like she is moving even when actually becalmed. I read some where that "ships are the nearest things to dreams that hands have ever made." If so, *Lady Jayne* is truly a dream!

"Grab a chance" wrote Arthur Ransome wisely many years ago,"...and you won't be sorry for might-have-been". Nick's very practical book will inspire others to "grab a chance" making it possible for many more to first build and then sail their very own craft.

Tom Barker
*Garden Bay Sailing Club,* Founding President,
Garden Bay BC, Canada June, 2011

# Peak Moments

*"I must down to the seas again, for the call of the running tide
Is a wild call and a clear call that may not be denied."*
John Masefield

It happened at Lee Bay near Pender Harbour, seventy kilometres north of Vancouver along the spectacular, uniquely rugged coast of British Columbia. I had just over-turned the Flying Dutchman. While clinging to the centre board it reluctantly dawned on me - I was no longer twenty-five and I might need to give up the high performance Dutchman dinghy for a stable keel boat, more appropriate to my age.

Earlier that afternoon, the fine summer day, the sun, a few white caps, and a fresh breeze beckoned me to the Flying Dutchman moored at a buoy in front of our summer place. Unthinkingly I followed a familiar routine. After hoisting first the large, full size genoa and then the main I cast off and set the sheets. Immediately a sudden puff laid the Dutchman over on its side. Instead of quickly releasing the sheets I stubbornly fought back, scrambling, heaving my body weight over the high side, but to no avail. Over she went.

Not that this was anything new. During twenty-five years of sailing the Dutchman there had been many capsizing incidents. But this was different. Whereas in the past I would have been standing on the centre board before the burgee hit the drink, now my reactions were slowing and the hull, quickly filling with water, settled into the ocean.

The Flying Dutchman is a high performance racing dinghy designed to be sailed by two and even if fully capsized can easily be righted by skipper and crew and sailed dry in minutes after opening the large scuppers in the transom. Sailing alone that day, my weight was not sufficient to raise the sails and rigging out of the water. While wind, waves, and tide pushed the sorry spectacle toward the rocky shore, I contemplated the onset of old age. Helpfully, someone on shore called the Coast Guard and the message of a sail boat in trouble at Lee Bay went out on VHF.

Approaching the sharp rocks below Norm Lee's old place, mast first, I planned to swim ahead and catch the mast before it would strike the rocks. Great planning, except, for the unintended consequences! With my body weight leaving the centre board the Dutchman turned turtle, leaving me with no choice but to place my body between the rocks and the hull. The hull was heaving broadside to the chop and standing to my armpits in water I helplessly wondered what to do next. I could neither right the hull, nor let go. Mercifully, help soon arrived. A friendly boater exiting Agamemnon Channel rounded Daniel Point and having heard the Coast Guard's appeal for help headed straight for me and generously offered a tow back to the mooring buoy. Now, while riding the overturned hull, dragging sails and rigging straight down through the water below, it was time to reflect on my sailing future. I knew the neighbours would have watched the mishap with interest. My wife Jayne would be worried with concerns. It was humiliating and humbling.

I love sailing. Being one with the wind and waves is a unique and exhilarating experience. Sailing is an active sport full of intensity. Maximum performance demands constant observation of wind, waves, and appropriate responses from tiller to sail trim. The experience is never as intense as in a dinghy. Keel boats are forgiving, dinghies are not. High performance dinghies require split second decisions. The responses of seasoned dinghy sailors are automatic and come as natural as breathing. Also, for successful sailing, brain is as important as brawn. The interaction between sail trim, wind direction, and steering must be understood and memorized for each point of sail. By harnessing the raw forces of nature the sailor experiences oneness with them. While using such forces to great advantage, the sailor is also subdued and humbled by their enormity. The force of wind and water is never conquered, only used.

Sailing evokes wonder. The wind stalks across the water, you feel it, the sails catch it, the hull heels and then it moves, attaining speed as if by a mysterious hand. The paradox of wild acceleration while courting the risk of being capsized. Physics can explain such forces but not remove the mystery and wonder of the experience.

Sailing demands total attention. It mobilizes all faculties. The eyes concentrate not only on the waves and the tell-tale signs of gusts playing on the water, but must also follow the luffing and twisting of the sails, the unpredictable course of nearby boats and fellow sailors and the ever-present risk of running aground on nearby shores. The ears record the sound of waves, the wind, the sails, and the hum of the rigging. Then there is feeling. The feeling on the cheek of a change in wind direction or strength, or feeling the movement of the hull responding to wind and waves and sensing that she is running free, or not. In sailing all faculties are essential and must be pitched to perfection.

The intensity that sailing generates is difficult to overstate. While racing, all redundant talk is unwelcome. While constantly adjusting the angle of sails to wind to maximize the movement of hull through water, skippers are on occasion so focussed on steering as to hold their breath without knowing it. The payoff of total commitment is wonderful satisfaction. The intensity of sailing restores the soul. It is recreational because life's normal concerns and worries are crowded out. Utilizing the forces of nature to attain maximum performance is its own reward, whether the race is won or lost.

The memory of a peak performance stays vivid for a life time. For years we sailed Vancouver's English Bay out of the Jericho Sailing club. During the summer months, English Bay's strong, steady westerlies provide some of the finest sailing conditions around Vancouver. The best of those sailings are etched in my memory. These are the ingredients: an eighteen knot westerly; a wild, broad reach; a robust crew stretched out suspended from the trapeze; the skipper flung back over the gunnel, toes under the restraint strap; playing the tiller by falling off in gusts and coming up in lulls; fighting excessive heel by instantly moving the traveller leeward and narrowing the gap between main and genoa to lessen the drive of the sails. Under such conditions the Flying Dutchman will lift its bow, plane and take off.

Responding to every gust with a will and life of its own, the Dutchman attains speed of ten, twelve, even fifteen knots, smashing through the chop, white caps and spray, leaving crew and skipper drenched from crown to toe, the tension builds, the rigging hums, the craft strung like a violin vibrates as it approaches peak performance. *That is sailing!*

But now, atop the hull and humiliated, I wonder, "Will I ever experience such peak moments again?" Is it time to trade the sailor's perilous perch on the pitched deck for the safety of a park bench; to be a spectator instead of a participant?

Well, forget such melancholy thoughts; this story has a happy ending. The unhappy incident of capsizing, turning turtle, and being towed upside down started the quest that led to the perfectly designed, beautifully crafted, wooden Dragon christened *Lady Jayne*, in honour of my wife and boat building-widow, Jayne.

This book describes the journey of that quest. It is a journey that disclosed new and unique peak moments. The joy of acquiring new skills such as: working with brass flat bar, stainless steel; how to melt 2,400 pounds of lead wheel-weights for pouring into a Dragon's keel; learning how to roll a hull effortlessly; and what it takes to make beautifully crafted blocks, almost entirely out of wood, strong enough to stand up to enormous strain. Acquiring a new appreciation for all that can be done with wood through steaming and bending, understanding how to finish and preserve bright work (wood left clear to show the grain) to bring out the grain and mellowness of aged wood, to marvel at the perfectly uniform grain of a two hundred year old Sitka Spruce, that and more is the essence of the journey.

This book records, step by step, the actual construction of one particular wooden boat and the experience of one amateur boat builder, but the lessons learned have application for all back-yard wooden boat builders. In addition, since it is a record of practical advice and helpful hints gathered over a life time of working with wood, richly illustrated with expertly drawn sketches and pictures to capture every detail, the book is useful to all who love to work with wood, whatever the project.

Perhaps, you are building a wine rack and like to know how mahogany can be finished to bring out and preserve its rich grain and also withstand alcohol stains. Perhaps, your interest is learning to sharpen hand tools, or how to steam and bend wood. Perhaps ... this book is for you!

There is also much to learn from mistakes. I kept a list of errors, things that could have been done better, those that had to be re-done, and ideas that seemed promising when first conceived but proved useless when applied. It is all here, recorded for the reader's instruction and perhaps amusement.

Boat building with wood requires many different skills. In contrast, the modern lifestyle requires few skills. Today, hardly any products are home-made. What skills we have lost! From gardening, cooking, preserving, baking, sewing to home repairs and backyard mechanics we are pushed aside by mass produced, manufactured products and a service industry of specialists. Where is the all-round handy person of yesteryear? Specialization has narrowed, reduced and diminished us. There are fewer and fewer opportunities to be creative, to be useful, to display ingenuity or individuality and to experience the personal accomplishment that comes from making something from start to finish with your own hands.

Increasingly we inhabit an artificial world with virtual experiences crowding out what is authentic and human. Cut off from the natural world and each other, modern humankind needs to discover links to what is real, authentic, and substantial. Sailing on water in sun and weather in a wooden, self-built, low free-board hull is as authentic as it gets. Wood is a living substance; no two pieces are alike. The many different species, each with its own unique characteristics, provide endless variety and a rich field of study, enough to last a lifetime. Fibreglass is efficient, but wood is authentic and beautiful. It elicits admiration, wonder, awe. Fibreglass can be utilized but not loved.

Creativity with wood, that oldest, natural and most durable of building materials, discloses who we are, our rootedness in the creation and our privileged vocation as architects, builders and artisans. Ours is a culture of standardization. That standardization is imposed particularly by computer technology. Efficiency is its allure, but it flattens individuality. Wooden boat building is an antidote, accentuating the rich diversity of talent latent in each of us. It enlarges the person. It gives expression to a person's energies, talents and abilities. Taking on a project which demands innovation and near perfection discloses what you are capable of, what sort of person you are.

Stop the mindless drift toward observer and spectator status, reclaim your status as participant and player, architect and artisan! Escape the deadening effects of the McWorld. Discover your potential. Build your own boat, *in wood!* Stop worshipping at the temple of efficiency, embrace beauty, indulge mystery and wonder, learn to love wood, chart your own course, and build your own boat, *in wood!*

> "Efficiency of a practically flawless kind may be reached naturally in the struggle for bread. But there is a something beyond – a higher point, a subtle and unmistakable touch of love and pride beyond mere skill; almost an inspiration which gives to all work that finish which is almost art – which is art."
> Joseph Conrad

CHAPTER ONE

# PLANNING, DESIGN, COSTS, SKILLS

"By failing to prepare you are preparing to fail"
Benjamin Franklin

## Perfection No Accident

Building a wooden sail boat is a substantial, expensive, time-consuming project requiring detailed and thorough planning. We all know of incomplete, unfinished projects, dreams unrealized. Benjamin Franklin, who accomplished so much in his life, reminds us that with proper planning there is no need for failure.

Years before starting actual construction, think about it and talk about it. Consulting friends and others, especially those with boat building and boating experience, is an indispensable part of the planning. *Lady Jayne* would not be without the helpful and wise counsel of many whose advice I sought. Do not fear asking. Invariably boaters and builders, amateurs and professionals alike, give their time and knowledge willingly, even enthusiastically. Boat builders, perhaps particularly wooden boat builders, are a fraternity eager to swap their successes and failures, always ready to talk about their joy and pride.

During the winter months many, many days were spent in the library; particularly in the extensive wooden boat building section of the Victoria Public Library. In addition to books, consult boating magazines for current building practises, materials and the latest technology. Also, the internet is indispensable. For people world-wide, united by a singular, often obscure interest, such as 'how to build a wooden Dragon from scratch', the internet is a wonderful blessing. Endless information can be gathered to assist the planning process and the actual construction. Forums and chat lines populate web sites of the various National Dragon Associations. They share information about building methods, materials, and equipment. There is no more accurate and useful source of information than those whose judgment is informed by practical, hands-on, personal experience.

## Design

The first major decision you must make relates to boat type, class and design. Humankind has built boats for thousands of years, yet each generation, while building on that vast store of knowledge and expertise, challenges the past by developing new designs utilizing the latest materials, machinery and methods. This endless variety is a testament to human inventiveness and makes an interest in boats so rewarding. While following in their wake each generation also strives to surpass those who went before.

Ask yourself what design suits your needs. For me, the design question centered on a keel boat to make sailing less of an extreme sport, but not so stable as to render it dull. In addition, since Jayne does not enjoy cruising there was no need for a cabin with accommodations. Form follows function. Having established what kind of boating and sailing you want (function) leads to the type and class of boat best suited to your needs (form). A lively, even tender, day-sailor suitable for racing seemed best for me. Also, I would be sailing in the relatively protected waters of the Georgia Strait between Vancouver Island and the British Columbia mainland.

The Georgia Strait can suddenly develop rough conditions with a short, steep chop, but safe harbour and anchorage are plentiful and seldom far away. With modern communication tools and mostly accurate marine forecasts there is no need to be out in heavy seas. For my purposes a relatively wet boat was acceptable. Finally, I wanted a design capable of being sailed solo, so as to not always be dependent on others.

I settled on the Dragon. The Dragon not only meets my needs as listed above, it also has two appealing and outstanding features - beauty and functionality. The lines are exquisite, traditional, sleek and slender similar to Lunenberg's *Blue Nose*, and the *J-Boats* of America's Cup fame from the 1930's. The sleek hull's long overhang both fore and aft make it arresting to the eye. People never fail to notice and remark on the Dragon's simple, yet striking beauty. It is like a whale, designed for life in water. *Lady Jayne's* pleasing appearance always elicits heartfelt compliments.

Secondly, the Dragon class has a proven track record of superior performance. It is not the fastest sail boat. Not at all! Along our coast, average speed ranges from four to six knots. But it is a lively boat and yet handles well. It sails remarkably close to the wind and lies steady. The Dragon heels easily and heeling increases its speed since it lengthens the water line without increasing the total wet area of the hull.

Anything of beauty is a joy forever. Where superb functionality is added to beauty it results in class and distinction, as well as joy. Such joy is more intense when the product is crafted with your own hands, when you see that it works well, each part answering the purpose for which it was made and when the whole embodies one's total energy and capability. That is satisfaction!

### Dragon Specifications

| | |
|---|---|
| LOA | 8.9 m |
| Beam | 1.95 m |
| Displacement | 1700 kg |
| (*Lady Jayne* fully rigged is closer to 1900 kg) | |
| Mainsail | 16 m2 |
| Genoa | 11.7 m2 |
| Spinnaker | 23.6 m2 |

Johan Anker, a noted Norwegian designer, builder and sailor, designed the Dragon in 1928 and it attained immediate international acclaim, particularly in the Scandinavian countries from which it spread to Germany, the Low Countries and Great Britain. Within ten years it attracted enthusiasts across much of Europe. In 1937, the Clydes Yacht Club in Britain awarded its much coveted Gold Cup to the Dragon class. Today, the International Dragon Association lists twenty six countries with national Dragon associations. In spite of its age, the Dragon's popularity remains undiminished placing it among the world's leading keel boats. From 1948 to 1972 the Dragon was raced in the Olympics and is one of the few classes to enjoy a popular following outside of the Olympics. As a child growing up in Holland after WWII, I recall seeing the Royal families of Sweden, Norway, Denmark, Holland, Belgium, Luxemburg, and England all sailing and racing Dragons. Is building and owning the Dragon a commoner's revenge against royalty?

## Cost in Time

Building, operating and owning a boat is expensive. Before embarking on a building project it is well to count the cost, both in money and time. Before I started, my understanding of costs in time and money were very vague and both turned out to be much greater than anticipated.

Few will be able to accurately estimate the time commitment. Only those who have direct, personal experience appreciate what is involved. During the construction it would amuse me to note the reaction of those who came to visit and look over the project. Most would take a peek at the hull in progress, offer some obligatory compliments and disappear in fifteen minutes, or less, but not those with experience building wooden boats. Persons with personal experience in boat building would keep circling the project, ask pointed questions, get down on their hands and knees, offer helpful suggestions and be lost to the world for the next hour or two.

About three years into the project, Aedgard Koekenbakker spent two and a half days with me. At the time Aedgard was sailing a forty-footer of his own design and make to Alaska and was in his fifteenth year of sailing solo all around the world. Before that he had been project manager for *Flyer*, the Dutch entry that twice won the Whitbread around the world race. In prior years Aedgard owned and operated the European franchise for British mast manufacturer - Proctor. He also knows the Dragon class intimately.

During those two and a half days, we talked boat building and boating and nothing else, often into the wee hours of the morning. Over a table strewn with the Dragon drawings, hastily drawn sketches, and supplier catalogues we discussed every aspect and challenge – deck construction, the finish of the wood, the layout of sheets and blocks, their type and construction, the rigging and mast construction, glues and epoxies, the seats and cockpit, sails, radios, GPS, trailers, moorage, and storage. I took copious notes and benefited greatly from Aedgard's seasoned advice. But I still marvel that it was possible for us to spend that length of time talking about this project and nothing, absolutely nothing, else.

I started construction in September 2000 and launched *Lady Jayne* late July, 2006. The period of six years was not entirely devoted full time to the project. Even though I was not gainfully employed, other interests and volunteer work took me away from *Lady Jayne*, particularly during the fall and winter months. It is not only the work but also the need to shop for obscure, unusual items and to research suitable materials and techniques, finding the correct information and advice, all of it consumes much time.

Too busy to care, I did not keep a record of hours worked, but since for about five months each year I put in time and a half and during the other months a considerable portion of my time, six years is not far off the mark.

Six years out of my life, for a boat? Such a daunting undertaking may seem too much for most. Perhaps, but to me it was a joy, a hobby, and never considered work.

Also, it is best to not speculate about the expected time of completion. Whenever I made short term predictions about a particular job, such as 'this sanding should be done by next week', invariably it would take three times as long. When planning and deciding whether to undertake this project know that it is labour intensive, that the work cannot be rushed, and that you will likely be consumed by it.

## Cost in Money[1]

If construction takes six years, expenses do not come all at once. That is the good news. The bad news is that anything related to a boat tends to cost more. The market is limited and specialized, particularly for a more traditional wooden boat. For example, since most modern boats are fibreglass and stainless steel, it is difficult to find bronze fittings. When I shopped for a bronze goose neck to attach a wooden boom to a wooden mast the best price was $750.00 (US) at an American foundry. To me, that

---

1     Unless otherwise noted, dollar amounts are Canadian, current at the time without adjustment for inflation.

was a lot of money for just one fitting. The result is inventiveness. In the end, the goose neck was made of Purple Heart, it looks fittingly traditional, it costs but a fraction, weighs less, and it functions wonderfully well.

At every step I considered costs very closely and whenever feasible made an item myself, or acquired it second-hand. Still, the costs mount. I have kept every invoice and recorded all expenses. In total, not counting my labour, electricity, insurance, and storage, *Lady Jayne* cost $28,534.32 and that includes: the sails ($2,500); a new, custom-built road trailer ($5,500); and a complete bow to stern cover ($1,750).

Do not think you are done with expenses once the boat is built. Operating expenses are an annual recurrence and can be substantial. The largest expense is for moorage and storage. In recent years, moorage costs have risen steeply reflecting the diminishing availability of good moorage. Costs can be severely trimmed if the boat is out of the water for most of the year, provided, of course, that on-land storage is available without charge.

In the off season, *Lady Jayne* is stored in the boat house on our property where she was built. Hence, for me the moorage cost is only three to four months in the summer. Those being the most expensive months for moorage it still adds up. The point is, before starting a project, inquire about availability and costs of moorage and storage.

Then there is annual maintenance. Each year, all bright wood needs at least one refresher coat of varnish and the below water surface needs one coat of bottom paint. Additional regular expenses include insurance for the boat, insurance and licensing for the road trailer if applicable, crane or launch ramp fees, membership in a yacht club or entry fees, oil and gas for the engine. Besides all that, unexpected costs for repairs must be counted on, even for a new boat. All hobbies and sports cost money and sailing like all boating is expensive. There is no escaping it, as the old saw has it, 'a boat is a hole in the ocean you pour money into.'

## What you must bring!

Before embarking on a building project of this scope it is prudent to add up costs in money and time, and if you can manage that, ask what skills are needed and how it compares to the skills you bring.

From my experience, successful, wooden boat builders of the home-made variety are handy with their hands. What their eyes see, their hands can do and fashion. It takes a ready facility with basic tools but also inventiveness and creativity. It helps to possess self confidence, no fear of failure, a positive frame of mind that turns problems into challenges.

I built *Lady Jayne* after acquiring a considerable amount of experience in both general wood working and boat building. My first boat building project was a Kitsilano 12, a sailing dinghy designed for home construction with a simple, hard-chine frame, covered with plywood and finished with a fibre-glass coating. Next, I did the finishing and rigging on the fibreglass Flying Dutchman. Then I completed a Peterborough, cedar strip canoe, followed by an Optimist built with plywood over a simple frame and painted.

The Optimist offers the best training in sailing for youngsters. The rocking hull-shape is protection against youthful mistakes and careless accidents. The Optimist will spin like a top rather than capsize. It is stable, safe, and great fun.

But in addition, the Optimist also offers the best training for beginner, wood boat builders. Its hard-chine design makes the work easy, yet there is some wood bending and plenty of trimming and fairing. These are important skills to acquire but the real payoff comes from the wonderful confidence and satisfaction a completed hull can give. Seeing your child or grandchild sail away in a seaworthy hull that you made from a few scraps of plywood and slats, will send your sense of self-worth soaring to new heights. If it weren't for being slightly sexist, I am almost inclined to quote Kipling, "... *you'll be a man my son.*"

While prior experience is helpful, it is not essential. A love for wood, a curiosity about all the uses to which it can be put, taking delight in the work, thoroughly enjoying all aspects of working with your hands, those are the essential ingredients. Skills can be learned but the drive to produce an artefact that is beautiful, functional, and an expression of your self must come from within.

"A musician must make music, an artist must paint,
a poet must write, if he is to be ultimately at peace
with himself. What a man can be, he must be."
Abraham Maslow

The Greek philosopher Plato held that happiness is to do what a person is uniquely fitted for. If you are fitted to be a farmer you'll be the best of farmers and you ought to be a farmer lest you miss your calling and purpose. If you are fitted to be a baker it means you are qualified, you'll bake the finest, and enjoy it. If you find boat building with wood deeply satisfying, it is because you are qualified for it, confirmed by the fine work you produce. It is your calling. You were made to be a wooden boat builder. It is what you are fitted for. As for the skills, you'll pick them up as you need them. Do what you most enjoy doing!

Do not be intimidated by the vast scope of the project stretching over many years. The enjoyment of a job well done sustains the inner compulsion to see the project through. Satisfaction comes at each step and provides motivation all along. Steam bending a hard piece of Oak into a fair curvature, sharpening a handsaw so it will cut without wandering, pushing a wood plane at the precise angle to create both a perfect wood curl and a straight, smooth edge on a rough board, the smell of Yellow Cedar, each is a source of immediate joy.

Do not practice delayed gratification! Take delight in the journey! The destination will bring its own reward. For now, drink in the satisfaction, the sense of accomplishment, the joy of producing a thing of beauty with your own hands from nothing but God-given raw materials.

"There is subtle charm about the thing that we have
made, and this is by no means always because of its intrin-
sic value, but because we have made it ourselves.
There is always something in it of our own, a distinctive something that
we imprint upon it, an individual stamp that we have put upon it."
Don Postema

# CHAPTER TWO
# *SHOP, SHARPENING, STEAM BOX*

"There is nothing – absolutely nothing – half so much
worth doing as simply messing about in boats — or
with boats ... In or out of 'em, it doesn't matter."
Kenneth Grahame

After carefully planning what type of boat meets your needs, and considering the cost in money and time, your own abilities, the availability of construction space, storage and moorage you may think you are ready to buy supplies and start building. Well, not yet! First comes a time of extensive preparation. Drawings have to be obtained, studied, understood and perhaps modified. A construction site to last for many years has to be planned and secured, the required tools and equipment have to be procured, special jigs, forms and patterns need to be prepared.

## Drawings and Registration

Working drawings for the Dragon may be purchased from the International Dragon Association[2] in London, England.

---

2     http://www.intdragon.org/

They consist of seven, 1320 mm x 813 mm sheets, and include the following:

- Construction Plan Wood (scale 1:10)
- Construction Plan G.R.P. (scale 1:10)
- Sail and Rigging Plan (scale 1:20)
- Hull and Keel Offsets (scale 1:5)
- Keel Sections & Detail of Heel (scale full size)
- Finished Keel Templates (scale full size)
- Template Plan (scale various)

Become fully familiar with the project, study the drawings at length and do not stop until every detail is understood. During the building it is imperative to always comprehend and anticipate what comes later and how that will fit with the particular piece or segment under construction at the time. While this may seem plain, common sense, remember, this warning is the fruit of my own mistakes, recorded later.

A complete set of drawings will show all the lines and all the dimensions but these drawings are not a how-to manual with step-by-step instructions. There are no instructions on how and in what order construction is to proceed, what kind of materials to use, how to fasten the various members, whether the hull should be carvel-built, clinker-built, plywood, or cold-molded, and at what thickness, or how many screws in what size to place where. Before construction can begin all the relevant questions must be settled. This is the time of preparation, a time to consult widely. In addition to all available books, consult friends, experts, library holdings, the internet and especially if you are near a Dragon fleet, look them over, see what others have done, and talk to the owners.

To qualify as a Dragon and receive a registered number there are weight limitations that must be observed and critical hull, sail and rigging dimensions must be within a 6 mm tolerance. While the Dragon Association's specifications allow for some options and limited deviations, overall, the rules are very strict. For example, *Lady Jayne* does not qualify for registered status because she has a 5hp, inboard engine. To me, the auxiliary power is very important. The entrance to Pender Harbour is narrow, subject to strong tidal currents, heavy boat traffic and unpredictable winds. It is no place to be without power. In such an instance, planning for where and how to place the engine has to be settled before any construction commences.

And placing an outboard bracket on such a distinctive stern would be obscene – a sacrilege.

Deciding not to register *Lady Jayne* allowed me to make additional modifications to suit local needs and personal preferences. Since there is no hoist capacity nearby, *Lady Jayne* needs to be launched from a trailer on a ramp. This requires taking the mast down. So, I modified the drawings such that the mast would not penetrate the deck but be mounted on top, supported by a pulpit. Also, it was my preference to slightly enlarge the cockpit for more comfortable seating. I eliminated the spinnaker from the sail plan and designed a very simple sheet layout plan that places the winches and nearly all sheets below deck. It lessens the clutter, and makes for a tidy, clean appearance showing the lines and bright finished wood to full advantage. I sacrificed a little speed, but a boat suited to local conditions and my personal preferences is worth it.

To register and obtain a number requires a fee and the cost of obtaining a certificate from a Marine Surveyor to confirm that all the dimensions and other requirements have been complied with. Official registration offers distinct advantages, such as enhanced re-sale value and the qualification to participate in the one-design Dragon sailing competitions, world-wide. In 2007 there were approximately 1,500 Dragons registered with the National Dragon associations, world-wide and it is estimated that there are an equal number of Dragons not registered, such as *Lady Jayne*. To register or not is a personal decision but it needs to be made before starting construction.

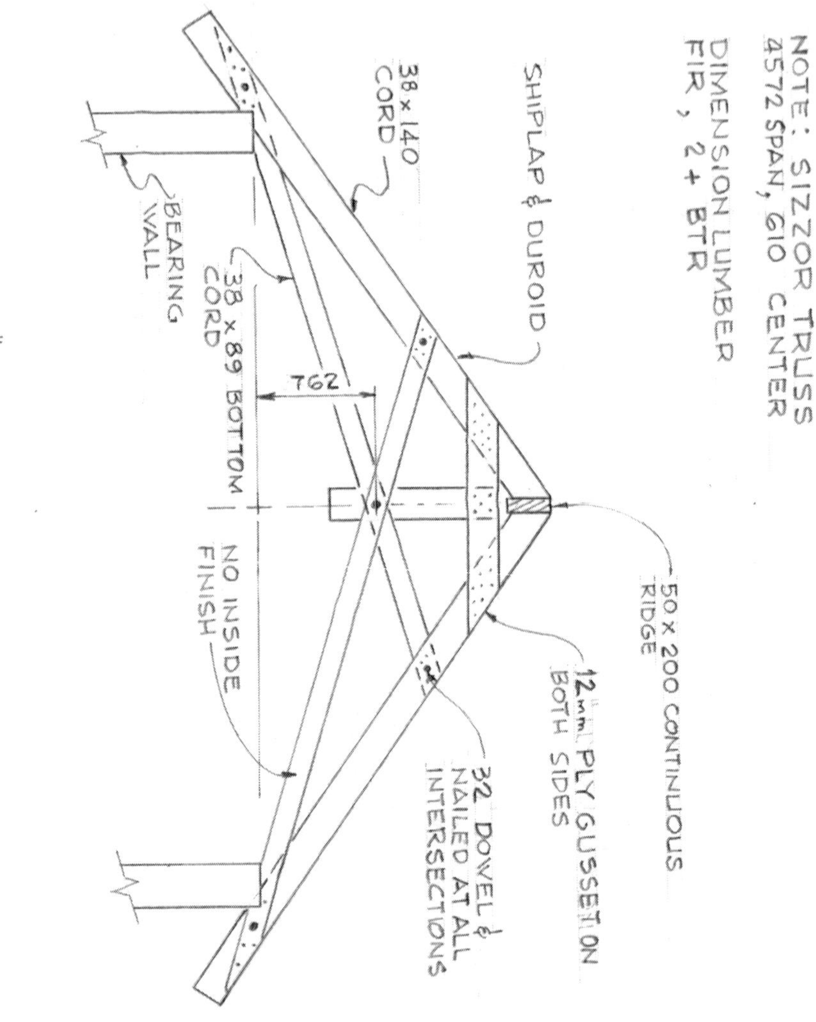

NOTE: SIZZOR TRUSS
4572 SPAN, 610 CENTER

DIMENSION LUMBER
FIR, 2 + BTR

SHIPLAP & DUROID

38 x 140
CORD

38 x 89 BOTTOM
CORD

762

NO INSIDE
FINISH

BEARING
WALL

FIG.#2 SCISSOR TRUSS.

50 x 200 CONTINUOUS
RIDGE

12mm PLY GUSSET ON
BOTH SIDES

32 DOWEL &
NAILED AT ALL
INTERSECTIONS

## Boat House and Workshop

I have a fine workshop in the basement of our summer home that is large enough to hold the table saw, lathe, thickness planer, steam box, drill press, and band saw. There is also room for the lofting and construction platform, a work bench and space to store materials. But I still needed a place to build and afterwards to store *Lady Jayne*. Fortunately, there was sufficient room for a boat house to be added to the back side of the summer home. Ideally, a boat house should be sufficiently large to also house the workshop area. If not, the distance between the two should be minimal for during the construction period you will walk that distance thousands of times.

My boat house is eleven metres by four and half metres, just big enough, but 60 cm wider would have been better. The length was determined by the length of the mast which is just over ten metres, above deck. Along one length of the boathouse are special brackets at 2 meter intervals, about 225 mm out from the wall and one metre up, to construct, and later to store the mast. Along the opposite length is one entrance door and the remainder has a built-in work bench about 510 mm out from the wall, eight metres long with shelving below and above.

Along the front of the bench are five retractable brackets, about one and one half metres apart (fig. 1). These brackets proved to be valuable for firmly holding long, thin boards while shaping with a wood plane or sanding them. They are well-constructed and are able to withstand much abuse. When not in use they slide underneath the bench, out of the way.

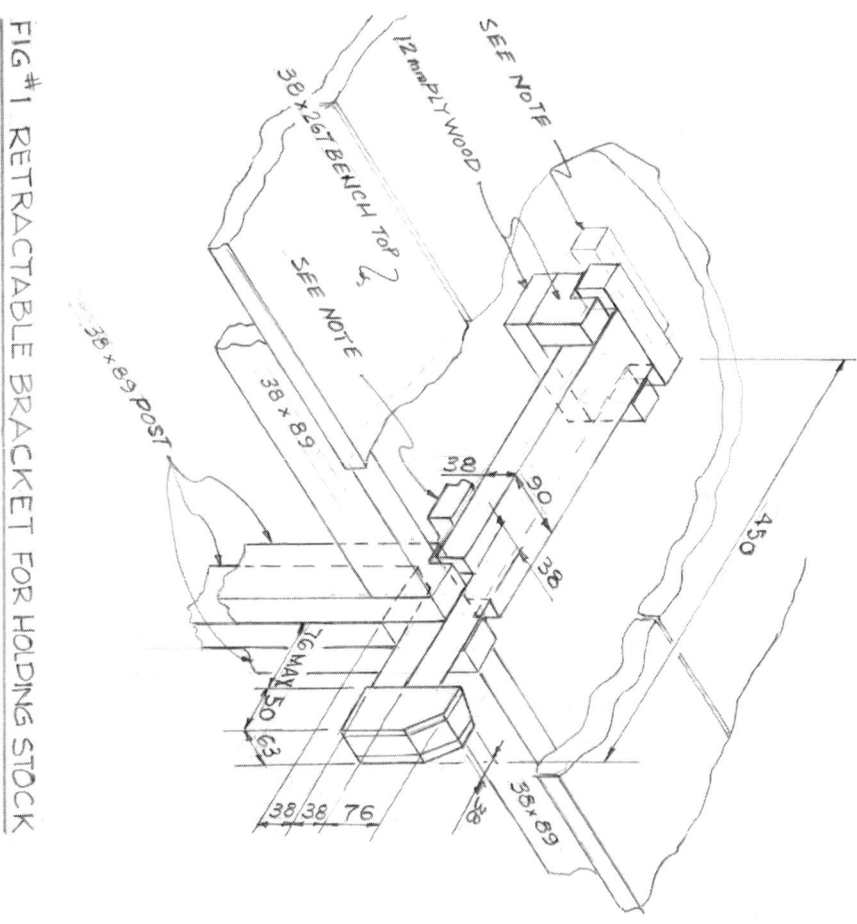

FIG #1 RETRACTABLE BRACKET FOR HOLDING STOCK

NOTE: WHEN NOT IN USE BRACKET CAN SLIDE UNDERNEATH BENCH.

38 x 267 BENCH TOP

SEE NOTE

12 mm PLYWOOD

SEE NOTE

38 x 89 POST

38 x 89

SEE NOTE

38 x 89

450

38

90

38

76 MAX

50

63

38 38 76

38

The simple scissor truss (fig. 2) for the roof serves two purposes. It is extremely strong and rigid but it also gives added head room, a wonderful bonus when working on the boat during the winter months. The dowels at the intersections make the truss doubly strong but the local building inspector had never seen a scissor truss and asked for an engineer's certificate. I could do without such unnecessary costs, told him so, and have ignored the letters of threats that followed.

The floor is sand and gravel with a sprinkling of fine gravel firmly packed on top. That saves the cost of concrete but it is also more practical. Occasionally during construction, and perhaps in the future for needed repairs, it is necessary to dig down to create space under the keel. Also, a boat house gets notoriously dusty. You don't want to varnish in a place where every movement raises a cloud of dust. Hence, prior to varnishing I bring in the garden hose to vigorously clean shop, spraying every surface from the rafters down. The ground absorbs the water and a few days later, although the floor surface may still be a little damp, conditions are ideal for working with varnish.

Finally, standing for hours on a firmly packed fine gravel surface is less tiring on the feet and back than concrete. If desired, heavy duty packing cardboard can be placed along the work bench, it makes working at the bench for long hours more kind to the feet and back than concrete. This is a personal report, not a scientifically proven fact but I know many others who concur.

"For grace with performance, few designers have bettered the Dragon,
so well-balanced that it will tack with the tiller untended,
so beautifully proportional that it never fails to turn admiring heads."

Anonymous

Inscribe these words on a plaque and prominently display it in the boathouse to lift sagging spirits when the going gets tough and tedious.

Before leaving the boat house, I should explain how to raise a power pole by yourself, in case you ever need to do so. Constructing the boat house required replacing a power pole supporting the service to our home from the road. It was best to incorporate the new pole into one of the corners of the boat house. The beach out front provided a fine Douglas fir pole and this was inched up to the building site with a heavy-duty come-along. Now the challenge was to lift the pole, prior to any other construction save the foundation, and place it on the concrete foundation in its precise location. It was done as follows:

- Lay the pole on the ground, with butt end at the spot it is to occupy, and ninety degrees to the foundation wall. This pole was so heavy, once it started to lift the butt end stayed in place without securing it.
- Secure a brace, three to four metres long, at the pole's butt end and along the foundation, or in line with the foundation. Then from the far end of that brace run another brace back to the pole at forty five degrees. The point where the two braces intersect at the foundation must be secured to prevent that point lifting or moving, but it must pivot when the pole is lifted.
- A similar, second set of braces is mounted on the pole at a ninety degree angle to the first.
- In my case, two nearby trees allowed for some blocks and rope to be rigged between the top of the pole and the trees with the running end fastened to the bumper hitch of a car. Drive away slowly and watch the pole come up till it reaches an upright position, there it is stopped by the second set of braces. It is best to stop the car at that point. (fig. 3)

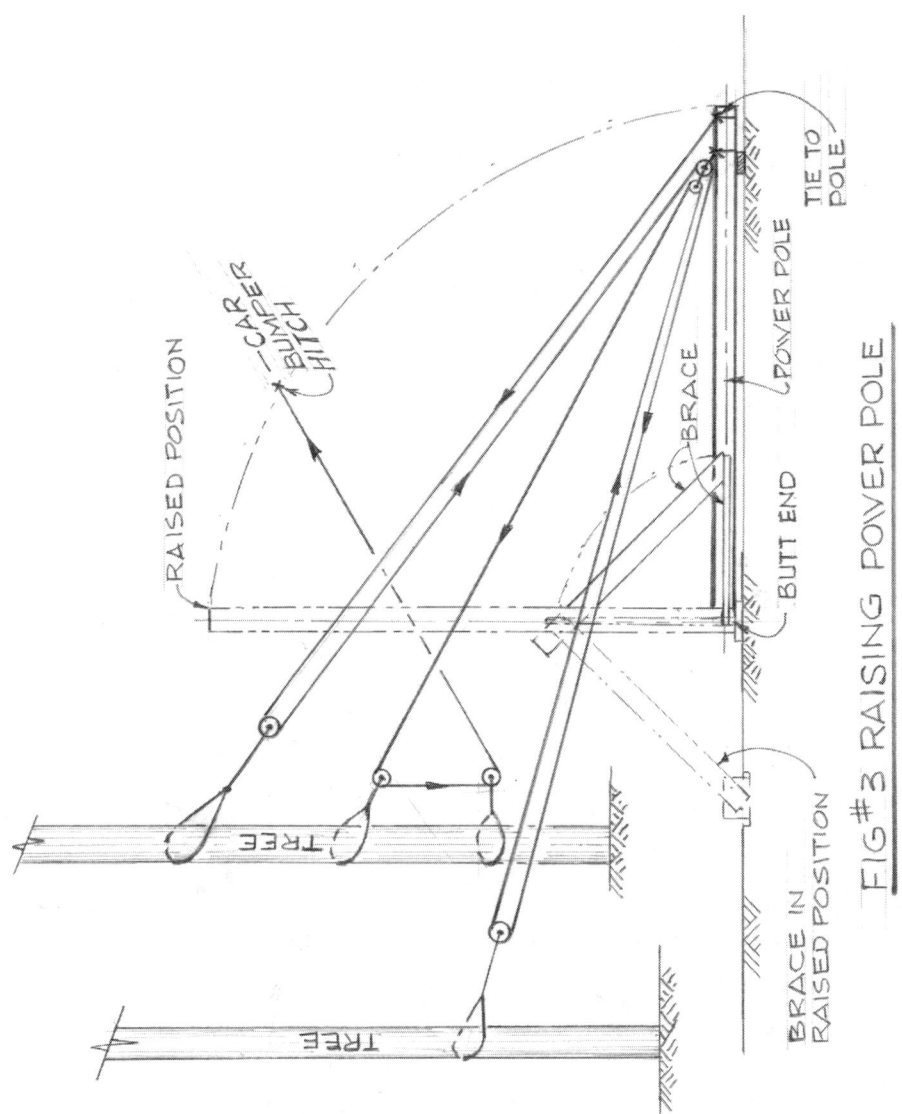

RAISED POSITION

CAR BUMPER HITCH

TREE

TREE

BRACE IN RAISED POSITION

BUTT END

POWER POLE

TIE TO POLE

BRACE

FIG #3 RAISING POWER POLE

## Tool sharpening

Chisels, wood planes, and hand saws need to be kept sharp. It is impossible to produce quality work without sharp tools. Sometimes it is difficult to break off work for an hour or two of sharpening. It seems like a non-productive interruption, but it is not. The reward is felt immediately by producing higher quality work, with less effort and in less time.

There are many sharpening techniques and most wood workers have their own favourite methods. Books have been written on the subject. It is wise to consult widely. I don't claim superior knowledge or skills but will simply record here what works for me. It is the result of trying various methods over many years.

## Chisels and wood plane-knives

Requirements are as follows:

- Bench grinder with a 150 mm or 200 mm by 25 mm,
  80x white aluminium oxide wheel. Such cool grinding wheels prevent turning the tool "blue".
- An adjustable stand independent from the grinder on which to rest the tool. (picture)
- I use an oil stone mounted in a portable platform (fig. 5), but
  the more recent Japanese water stones and also the diamond
  stones are excellent. When not in use the oil stone is protected
  with a snugly fitted wood cover to keep off dust and dirt.
- A honing guide to steady the tool for the final edge.
  You can buy these but they can easily be made by using an abandoned bicycle wheel axle (fig. 5).

Start the sharpening process by removing a very small amount of steel from the back of the tool along the cutting edge by holding the back-side of the tool flat against the side of the grinding wheel. (The grinding wheel must run absolutely true, if not, adjust till it is true.) Then, remove some steel from the cutting edge to eliminate all nicks and gouges and produce a straight edge at ninety degrees to the sides of the tool. This is done by placing the cutting edge against the side of the wheel but this time at a ninety degree angle to the wheel and holding the back of the tool up. The purpose of holding the tool's back side up is to have the burr form on the cutting edge, which still needs sharpening. Hold a set-square against the side and the sharp edge to ensure the cutting edge is square to the sides.

Adjustable stand. Tool-rest slides on tubes

The adjustable stand is placed in front of the grinder and clamped down to the workbench. The chisel or plane-knife is placed in the tool-rest that rides on the adjustable stand. First, the distance to the wheel is determined and the tool is secured to the platform with the two wing nuts. Then, the angle of the cutting edge is determined and secured with the two wing nuts on the adjustable stand. What should that angle be? That depends on what the tool is expected to do. Again, there are many theories but the simple, practical advice is this: for cutting across the grain and for removing large quantities of stock use a low angle, while for cutting with the grain, and for removing minute quantities of stock use a higher or more acute angle.

With the grinder turned on, all that remains is to gently and slowly ride the tool-rest along the tubes of the adjustable stand such that the cutting edge of the tool will move from right to left and back along the width of the grinding wheel. Planting your feet firmly, and a little apart, hold the tool-rest with both hands and while sliding it back and forth with an even, constant motion, apply gentle downward pressure on the tool.

After five or six passes, take a look. The grinding wheel should be removing steel along the cutting edge surface such that the new cutting edge surface is at first parallel to and finally perfectly even with the back side of the tool. If not, adjust accordingly. As you approach that final edge apply less downward pressure. By holding the cutting edge up to a light you'll see how much the cutting edge and the back of the tool are still apart. When all of the flat area has been removed and the two surfaces meet perfectly the grinding part is finished. Going too far, produces a burr on the back side, particularly when grinding an acute angle. An ever so slight burr is acceptable and will be removed during honing on the oil stone, but too much burr can be remedied only by starting the grinding process all over.

The honing process is critical. This is where razor sharp edges are born or die.

Wet the stone, with oil or water, (depending on the type of stone) to prevent steel filings from clogging the surface. Start with the backside. Place the tool on the stone, back side down, with one hand pressing down firmly and evenly, pull the tool towards you in one gentle motion. Check to see that the back side of the cutting edge makes contact with the stone along the entire width of the cutting edge. If not, adjust your hold and the pressure on the tool. Make three or four passes.

Place the tool into the honing guide so that the cutting edge surface makes contact with the stone, in particular along the cutting edge itself. This is very critical. However, contact along the cutting edge only, produces too much burr along the back side. To find the correct angle takes trial and error. Once the angle has been set and the tool secured in the guide, hold the guide with both hands and move it such that the tool's cutting edge surface will be pulled towards you along the length of the stone under gentle pressure. Do this three times. Note: if the tool is wider than the stone, pull it across the stone and increase the number of passes accordingly.

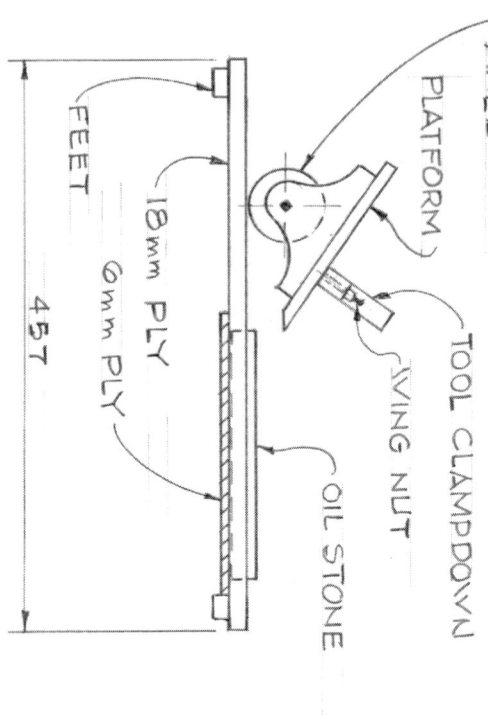

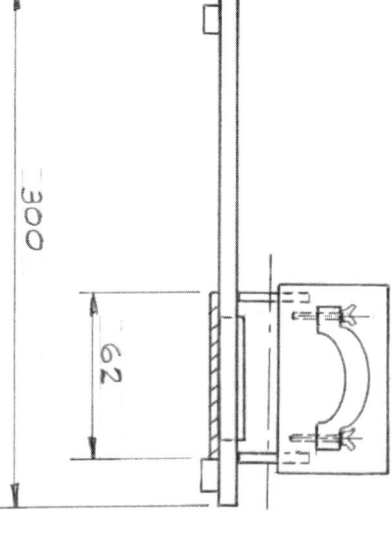

FIG #5 OIL STONE PORTABLE PLATFORM WITH HONING GUIDE
TO PUT FINAL EDGE ON CHISELS AND PLANE BLADES

BICYCLE WHEEL AXLE

PLATFORM

TOOL CLAMPDOWN

WING NUT

OIL STONE

18mm PLY

6mm PLY

FEET

457

300

62

Now test the edge against your thumb. I don't know of a better way. It allows you to feel where the burr is. If it is on the backside and a little pronounced you should bring the burr over to the front, or if the other way, bring it to the back. The burr is brought over by repeating a single pass of the honing process outlined above. Then test again. The burr should lessen and give way to a razor edge. If not, you may have to start all over. Time and practise make perfect. Do not expect to succeed immediately but these steps have a proven record and will work for you.

## Filing Hand Saws

Many people have at least one hand saw somewhere around their house, but sadly, even among wood workers, few of those saws are sharp enough to cut well, or at all. Increasingly we rely on power saws of all kinds. However, boat building frequently requires a hand saw for otherwise inaccessible places. Also, a needle-sharp saw takes less elbow grease than a dull one, but the real benefit is in what it does to wood. Instead of a saw that wanders and butchers the stock, a sharp saw cuts straight and clean, leaving a product to be proud of. Not infrequently, a hand saw produces more satisfying cuts then a less easily controllable power saw. Once you have used a well sharpened saw you'll not want to do without it. Filing a hand saw is easier than it seems. It does however take patience, attention to detail and practice. For those interested, detailed instructions are in the appendix.

## Building the steam box

After hours of sharpening tools, treat yourself to another fun job. Steam bending is to wooden boat building what wind is to a child's kite, they're inseparable. A steam box is simplicity itself. All you need is an electric kettle, some PVC pipe, wood, and insulation, the latter is optional. Nearly all the steaming for a Dragon is for stock less than two metres in length and 75 mm, or less wide. Hence, the steamer can be just over two metres long and inside 100 mm wide and 125 mm high. Provide a hinged opening on one end at least, or on both ends to permit steaming of short pieces of stock at each end and steaming a middle section of a longer piece of stock (fig.7).

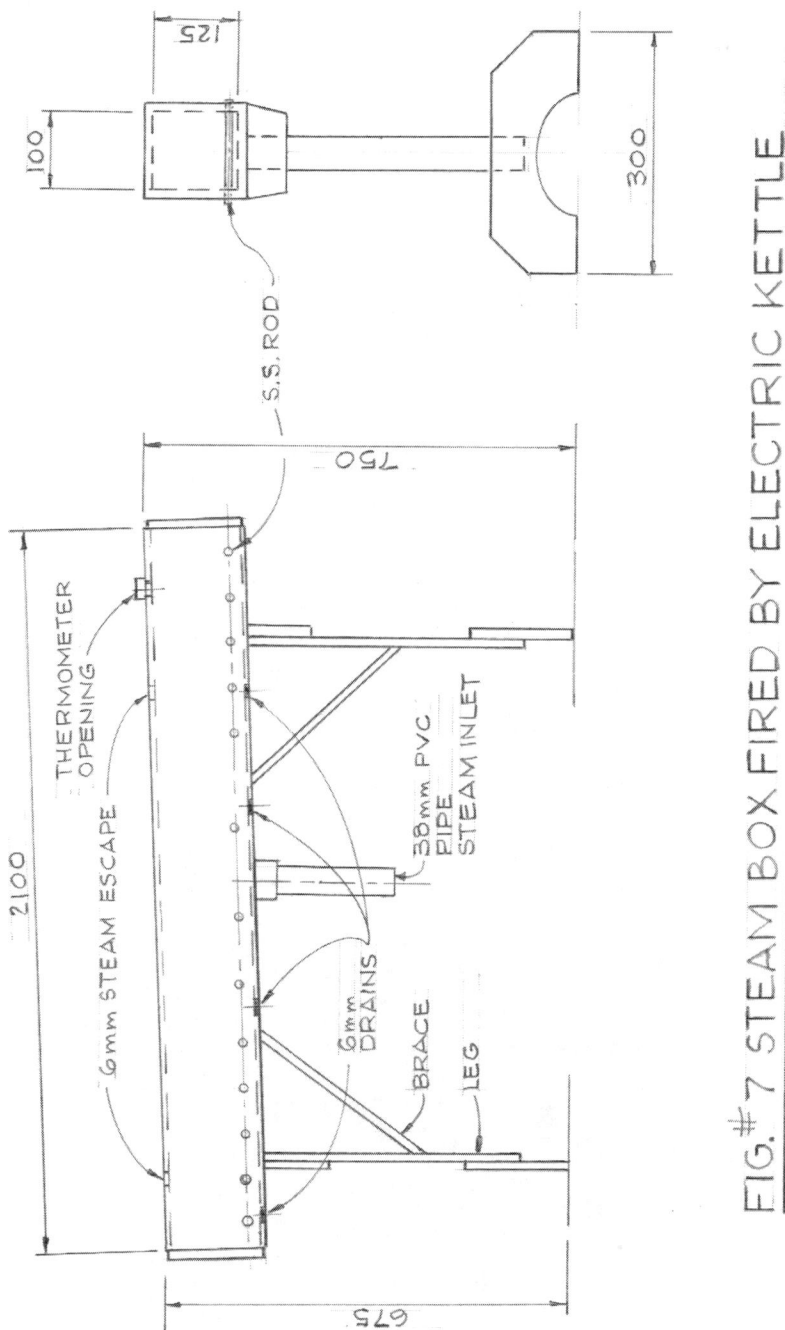

FIG.#7 STEAM BOX FIRED BY ELECTRIC KETTLE

S.S. ROD

THERMOMETER OPENING

6mm STEAM ESCAPE

6mm DRAINS

38mm PVC PIPE STEAM INLET

BRACE

LEG

125

100

300

750

2100

675

To allow a candy thermometer entry for reading the temperature cut a 25 mm diameter opening on top near one end. Also, drill two, 6 mm holes at each end for steam to escape. The steam now flows along the stock and in addition, the build-up of moisture is lessened. Provide some 6 mm holes in the floor for drainage and slope the box to allow moisture to drain away.

To keep stock off the floor and the steam circulating all around the stock, insert 6 mm diameter stainless steel rods through the sides just above the floor. For steaming short pieces, space the rods 150 mm on centre near the two ends and about 300 mm on centre in the middle section. To lessen rot, use Western Red Cedar. To save energy, wrap the outside in insulation. Western Red Cedar has one disadvantage – it can stain the stock. If that is a concern, do not lean stock against the insides of the box.

For a steamer this size, one kettle is sufficient. However, the deck on *Lady Jayne* requires bending, along the flat, four mahogany planks 75 mm wide, 5 mm thick and 5 metres long. Those are steamed in a 100 mm diameter length of PVC with two kettles and numerous 6 mm holes to get the steam moving along the stock. Similarly, the Yellow Cedar decking can be steamed in a 62 mm diameter length of PVC with just one kettle. Every part of the steam box must register temperatures within a few degrees of boiling – 100 degrees C. If that temperature cannot be reached and maintained at the ends of the box, an additional kettle is needed.

The steam box is simple and indispensable

## Bending Jigs

*L*ady *Jayne* requires a considerable amount of wood bending, therefore jigs are needed to hold the stock in place first for bending and then for laminating. About twenty simple jigs cut out of standard 38 mm by 140 mm common lumber will do for most of the bending. These jigs are screwed into position on the wood bending platform and used over and over to form the unique curvature of each of the ribs. A second jig is used for forming the coaming that surrounds the cockpit and cuddy. This is a ninety degree upright held in place by a plywood gusset, thirty of these are needed (fig.8).

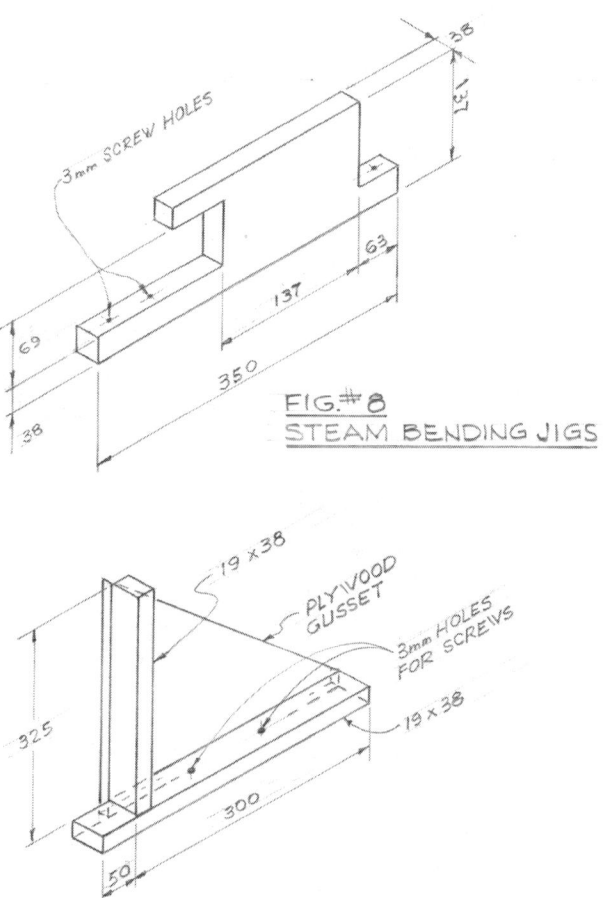

FIG.#8
STEAM BENDING JIGS

## Wood Lathe and Sander

The *Lady Jayne* requires some lathe work, for example, to turn the sheaves for the wooden blocks and to turn various sized dowels for plugs and other uses. In addition, the shaft to run the lathe is excellent for also driving a good-sized sanding wheel- which is very useful. There is no need to spend your life savings buying a lathe. Build one! The base and frame should be solid and substantial to minimize vibration during use. Don't make the base too narrow.

If space is a concern, it helps to have strategically located coasters that catch when the unit is lifted on one side. I have such coasters also on the band saw, table saw, drill press, and planer, making it easy to move such equipment close together and out of the way when not in use.

For the frame, use standard 38 mm by 140 mm and 38 mm by 89 mm softwood. However, the tail head and the gouging tool-rest must be able to slide along the carriage into location and be firmly clamped in place. To achieve this it is best to line the two, 38 mm by 89 mm that make up the carriage with 6 mm thick oak. Oak on oak greased with candle wax makes a slick, smooth runner and the candle wax will not collect sawdust and dirt.

Scrounging at the ABC Traders scrap metal yard in Richmond turned up a stainless steel shaft, 18 mm diameter by 300 mm long, with threading on both ends in place. Excellent, for the headstock mandrel! At the cost of scrap metal this was a steal.

Fit the shaft into bearings with a 100 mm by 18 mm inch sheave, or pulley, driven by a v-belt to a second-hand electric motor from an abandoned washing machine. Fit the motor with a multi-step pulley to vary the speed. A fine lathe for about $50 is within sight.

The headstock's outboard mandrel can be fitted with a 300 mm diameter sanding disk made of 25 mm thick plywood. The headstock's inboard mandrel drives the wood lathe by spinning the turning stock to be worked on. At this end the mandrel should be ground to a point and fitted with two stainless steel nuts held in place by being tightened against each other.

The outer nut needs to be modified on the bench grinder such that it leaves four sharp prongs that will grab the turning stock and drive it. The nut should be positioned such that the cutting points of the prongs are nearly 12 mm short of the mandrel's sharpened point. When turning stock is fitted between the headstock mandrel and the tailstock barrel, holes are drilled in the centre at the ends of the stock. The hole at one end receives the pointed end of the mandrel and serves to hold the stock in place, while the four prongs grab the stock and turn it.

The tailstock barrel is much simpler. It need not turn but in my case I used an abandoned bicycle axle and its bearings, so it too, turns. To place and hold the housing of these bearings I drilled holes, a little larger in diameter and deeper than the size of the housing and then embedded them in epoxy. The wooden tailstock is secured and held in place by a short, solid wedge tapped in place with a mallet against the underside of the carriage (fig.9). When properly fitted it holds exceptionally well.

Last, is the construction of the tool-rest. Its height should be even with the centre of the mandrel. It needs to be adjustable both along the carriage and in distance from the turning stock. For releasing and tightening the tool-rest I could have, again, used a wedge against the underside of the carriage but I chose instead a stainless steel 18 mm threaded rod with a turning nut on one end, embedded in a wood handle (fig.9). It too, works fine.

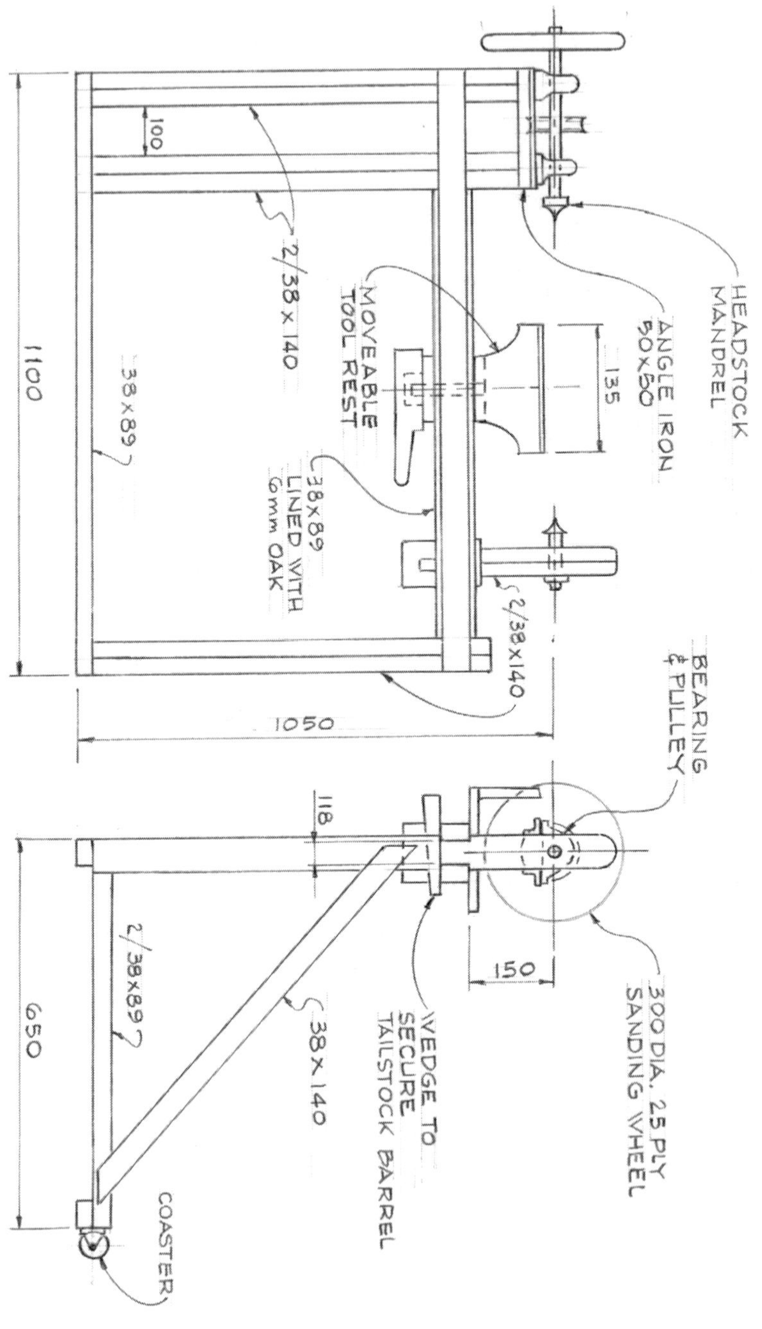

FIG. # 9 WOOD LATHE WITH SANDING DISK

HEADSTOCK MANDREL

ANGLE IRON 50x50

135

100

2/38 x 140

38x89

1100

MOVEABLE TOOL REST

38x89 LINED WITH 6mm OAK

2/38x140

1050

BEARING & PULLEY

118

2/38x89

650

150

WEDGE TO SECURE TAILSTOCK BARREL

38 x 140

300 DIA. 25 PLY SANDING WHEEL

COASTER

## Roller on Adjustable Stand

Your shop is now adorned with a home-made, wooden lathe and an untried steam box. You are itching to try them out. Well, there is a perfect project to test the lathe, your own turning skills, and the art of bending wood. If you have no experience in wood turning it is best to consult any standard wood turning manual to master the basic steps[3]. The project I have in mind is to turn some rollers. You will need several. I built three, 400 mm wide rollers on stands, adjustable for height, and at times needed all three when pushing long stock through the table saw, band saw or planer. The rollers were turned from Douglas fir branches pulled from a slash burning pile up the hill towards Sakinaw Lake behind our place. They dressed out at about 90 mm in diameter. (fig.10) For supports I steamed, bent, and laminated two strips 12 mm by 38 mm softwood but it is better to use more and thinner strips.

Better still, don't use softwood. Softwood is not very suitable for steam bending. However, if you use softwood use very thin strips. They bend easier and when laminated hold the shape better than two strips.

3      A very useful text covering all the basics: Woodturning, A Foundation Course, New Edition by Keith Rowley, Guild of Master Craftsman Publications Ltd. East Sussex, England, 1999.

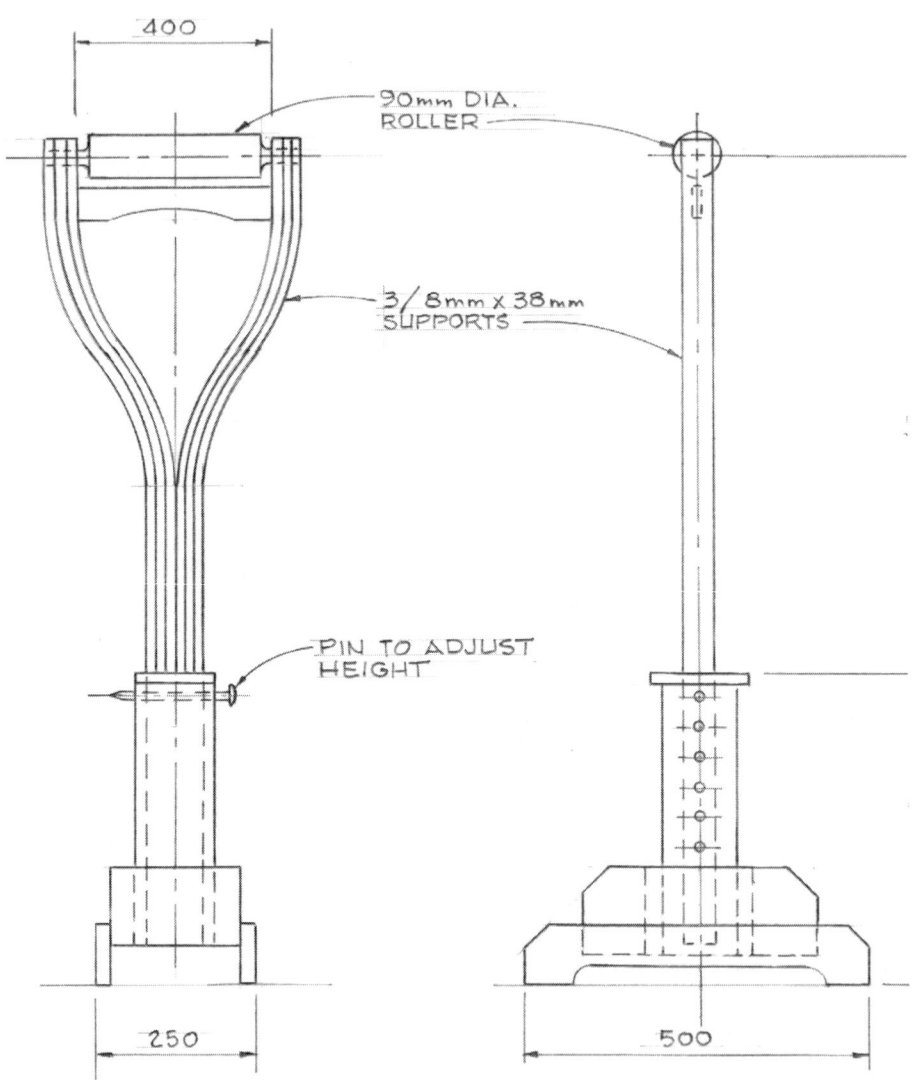

400

90mm DIA.
ROLLER

3/8mm x 38mm
SUPPORTS

PIN TO ADJUST
HEIGHT

250

500

FIG.#10 ROLLER ON ADJUSTABLE HEIGHT

## Sanding Blocks

It is useful to have three or four sanding blocks, each with its own grit to lessen the number of times sanding paper must be changed. To fit pre-cut sheets, make the blocks 77 mm by 230 mm by 9 mm thick. Cut a handle-grip on the band saw and shape it with a router. Cut two pieces of flat aluminum 15 mm wide by 75 mm long to hold paper in place. Secure the aluminum with one stainless steel carriage bolt and a wing nut for easy removal when replacing the sanding paper sheets.

## Clamps

It is often said that in boat building one can never have enough clamps. Regretfully, I discovered this truth more than once. I have an assortment of about forty store-bought clamps in all sizes, mostly c-clamps, some pipe clamps, and some bar-clamps, four of which have a four feet bar. In addition, I made fifteen wooden clamps using 9 mm by 200 mm galvanized carriage bolts. The jaws are made of 38 mm by 38 mm oak, 180 mm long.

The carriage bolt should be threaded most of the way and placed 75 mm from one end. In one of the jaws the bolt is fitted very snugly and driven in place, the other jaw should move easily along the bolt. A block of 18 mm stock is placed between the jaws at the very end nearest the bolt. The length of the block is equal to the thickness of what needs to be clamped. The bolt's nut is tightened against a flat washer to close and put pressure on the jaws.

Also, a ClampTite tool is indispensable both for construction and maintenance of any boat. This little tool will tightly and neatly wrap wire around an object and effectively lock it in place. It can be used around pipe, hose, and rope in a wide range of dimensions and for a variety of purposes; for example, to temporarily clamp a round object while the glue dries or permanently attach a hose to a bilge pump. ClampTite is available at marine suppliers or over the internet.

## Shaper

I don't have a shaper but I do have a hand-held router. It is easy to build a little platform to mount the router so it does double duty as a shaper. It takes a chunk of 18 mm plywood about 600 mm square. Drill a 63 mm diameter hole in the middle and fix the router on the underside so the cutter comes up through the hole. Most routers have a shoe held in place with three or more small bolts. Remove the shoe and use the bolt holes with longer bolts to fasten the router to the underside of the plywood platform. To prevent any movement let the router into the plywood with a rabbet about 6 mm deep. If that is not possible, fit another piece of 12 mm plywood snugly all around the router. Fasten two pieces of 38 mm by 89 mm on the underside, one on each side, long enough to rest on the workbench and have the router suspended from the platform just in front of the bench. Clamp or screw the 38 mm by 89 mm on the bench. The router turned into a shaper is complete. For each job and cutter an appropriate fence is needed and screwed to the platform. It works best if there is absolutely no movement in the platform or the router. As with any shaper, watch your eyes and especially your fingers!

## Epoxy Measuring Cups

There are mainly two suppliers of epoxy – the well-known *West System* from the eastern US and *System Three* from Seattle (previously *Industrial Formulators*, Burnaby, BC, Canada). They provide nearly identical products and because of the local connection I used *System Three*. Technical information was thorough and prompt. There are many different types of epoxies for various wood types, temperatures and applications. These are all explained in their catalogue and technical literature. One bit of advice; you will need large quantities of epoxy, therefore buy in bulk. I bought in 12 litre units a total of 36 litres but should have bought one, 30 litre unit at a much better price.

The construction process requires measuring and mixing hundreds, of mostly small, even very small quantities of epoxy. Epoxies consist of two parts, a resin and a hardener, that must be measured very accurately and mixed thoroughly for maximum bonding. Acquire a large quantity of small, clear plastic cups to mix these small quantities of epoxy.[4] Each cup can be used just once and is discarded after use.

For measuring purposes, a clean cup is placed inside one of a variety of clear plastic measuring cups. The resin and then the hardener, *always in that order*, are pumped or poured into the clean cup up to the relevant mark on the measuring cup and mixed thoroughly.

Measuring cups are prepared as follows:
- Cut out a 6 mm. wide slot vertically down the side of a cup by first drilling two, 6 mm. holes with a forstner bit to prevent shattering the plastic. One hole near the bottom and one near the rim. Then cut the plastic in two straight lines between the holes with a utility knife.
- Take a second cup and put some liquid such as water into it, place the cup inside the measuring cup and mark the water's level on the measuring cup with a *Sharpie* marker.
- Fill yet another cup with water to exactly the same mark, empty both quantities of water into one cup and again mark the water's level on the measuring cup. These two marks are sufficient for

---

4    I experienced an unfortunate incident the first time I mixed *System Three* S-1 Sealer. This epoxy dissolved the plastic mixing cup. I then used a glass jar. It never happened with any other epoxy product that I used. Later, I used S-1 in plastic squeeze bottles without any problem. Before using plastic cups and laying up a large store it is prudent to do a test run.

measuring epoxies with a one-to-one ratio by volume. Make any number of such measuring cups for a range of different volumes.

- Most epoxies use a two-to-one ratio by volume. To accommodate those, make additional measuring cups with three incremental marks, each increment containing the same volume of liquid.

## Lofting Platform

The lofting platform consists of three, 1220 mm by 2440 mm sheets of 15 mm plywood or board configured into an 'L' shape with one 4.8 m leg and the other 2.4 m. I used 2440 mm long landscape ties about 610 mm on centre as a base. Next, on top of the landscape ties fasten 38 mm by 89 mm on the flat at 610 mm on centre, then, fasten the plywood sheets on top. The platform should be level and straight in all directions. Since you will loft or draw the exact shape and curvature of each of the fifteen hull stations in actual size on this surface there will be a multitude of criss-crossing lines. To prevent confusion, it is best to paint the surface in white with at least two coats of high gloss good quality paint.

## Drawings Table

Throughout the construction period the drawings will be in constant use. It is best to construct a simple, elevated, slanted support where the drawings remain permanently. Mount the most used sheets such as the Construction Plan and Sail and Rigging Plan on rigid, light weight material such as core plastic board to be easily lifted while the less used sheets are placed underneath and can be rolled to one side like a scroll when the ones underneath need to be consulted. I found this arrangement practical for quick access, and it kept the drawings in perfect condition. The dimensions of the main surface should be large enough to provide space on both sides of the sheets for pencils, erasers, rulers, set-square, and protractor.

## Power Tools

In addition to the portable router and lathe/sanding wheel, my workshop is equipped with the following power tools.

- A Craftsman 228 mm table saw bought fifty years ago and still in good shape.
- A Black & Decker 200 mm circular saw, also fifty years old.
- A 311 mm Delta thickness planer with a lift of 152 mm mounted on a home-made base and feeding table.
- A M.A.P. drill press with 12 mm bit capacity. An assortment of high quality drill bits ranging from 2 mm to 12 mm.[5]
- A Craftsman 355 mm band saw with 152 mm height.
- A Craftsman 200 bench grinder.
- A Makita 82 mm power plane. Not essential but handy to have.
- A good quality Porter Cable bayonet style jig saw.
- An old 150 mm Craftsman sander/grinder I use for very rough sanding and grinding.
- A Black & Decker cordless reversible drill. It is ideal to have two, one for drilling, and one for driving wood screws.

You may notice the absence of a power belt sander and an orbital sander. Except for the sanding wheel mounted on the wood lathe's outer mandrel, I prefer to do all sanding by hand with an assortment of sanding blocks. It is a personal choice. In my opinion, power belt sanders can gouge wood and leave an ugly mess. Orbital sanders for finishing are more easily controlled, but the best control is offered by a hand-held sanding block.

Purchasing quality tools is never an expense, it is an investment. Working with poor tools makes quality work difficult to achieve. Good tools last a lifetime and over time become treasured companions. Don't be niggardly when investing in tools.

---

5     Most drill bits on the market are not worth buying, particularly for use on stainless steel. I get good results with drills recycled from the aircraft industry available from BIT BY BIT, 5424 Monkey Tree Lane, Sechelt, British Columbia, V0N 3A2, www.bitlady.com

You have now made extensive plans on what to build, how it is to be built, where to build it and acquired the tools for the job. You have also mastered the art of sharpening those tools to keep them in good condition for quality work. All this planning bodes well for the future, a successful completion is almost assured. You are truly ready to cast off on a new journey of adventure and discovery.

# CHAPTER THREE

# LOFTING, STEAM BENDING, LAMINATING FRAMES

"Don't wait for your ship to come in. Row out to meet it."
Jackson Brown

Supplies and materials for wooden boat building are not readily available at every local hardware store. It is wise to plan ahead. The project stretches over many years. You will not need everything at once, but it is important to think ahead three months, even half a year, determine what is needed, research quality and price and then order well ahead to avoid disappointing delays. For example, while starting on the lofting, order enough White Oak for the frames, keelsom and stem.[6]

Most of this stock will need to be steamed and bent. It is difficult to steam-bend kiln-dried wood. It is best to use air-dried stock with moisture content of 15% to 25%. Explain to the supplier what the wood is to be used for and what moisture content you require. This is very important. Most readily available stock has been kiln-dried. Even air-dried stock that has been in storage for a long time may have a very low moisture content making it less suitable for steam bending.

Moisture content is difficult to reverse. Soaking kiln-dried and over-dried wood even for days is not much of a remedy. If possible find a source of air-dried stock with relatively high moisture content that makes it suitable for steam bending. If the moisture content of the wood is too low, the laminated layers must be significantly reduced in thickness. The point is, the best suited materials are scarce and planning ahead is a must.

---

6      I purchased most wood from P.J. White Hardwoods, Vancouver and West Wind Hardwood, Sidney. Their staff is knowledgeable.

## Lofting

The object of lofting is to draw the outer line of the frames at each station. These lines are drawn on the working platform in actual size. The lines are then used as the pattern to bend the ribs that will form the hull's shape and curvature. Each station will have one frame consisting of two ribs, one rib for starboard, and one rib for port. Each frame defines the hull's profile or unique cross-section at a particular station. The distance of each station from fore and aft is as per Construction Plan.

Lofting requires the following:
- Measure tape (in this case metric)
- Supply of pencils
- Pencil sharpener
- Ball point pens of different colours
- Flat steel straight edge (1220 mm)Wood straight edge (about 2200 mm) Test straightness by drawing a line along one side, turning it over to check that it matches perfectly.
- 25 mm, bright finishing nails.
- An assortment of thin, wooden battens of various lengths and widths to draw curves. For these battens select even, straight grain stock from Sitka Spruce, Yellow Cedar, Oak, or African Mahogany. The test is that they bend fair.
- For lofting alone, you will be on your knees for several days and may wish to invest in knee pads.

The Body Plan shows the cross-section of the hull at each station. The entire Body Plan needs to be reproduced in actual size on the working platform, except, whereas the Body Plan shows only one half of the cross-section at each station, both halves must be drawn on the lofting platform. The stations should be drawn within the 2.4m by 2.4m section of the working platform but in such a way that the Datum Line can be extended into the 4.8 meters section to allow (1) lofting the hull's stern and stem sections and (2) to project an extension of the mast into the workshop. The latter is needed to calculate the mast rake (see Mast Pulpit section Chapter Four).

Ideally, there is sufficient room beside the lofting platform to layout with a batten the section of mast from the deck to the top of the forestay (about 7100 mm). If not, an alternative area must be found, or the mast rake can be determined scaled down from actual size. The latter is not recommended since mast rake is crucial to hull performance and the Dragon's design does not permit easy rake adjustment after construction is completed. Laying out the actual size and measurements is preferred to scaling rake from the plans.

Lofting starts by drawing the grid from the Body Plan. The grid consists of the vertical Centre Line, the horizontal Datum Line and Water Lines, and the diagonal lines. These are first drawn in pencil against a straightedge, checked and re-checked, and if found to be absolutely correct, drawn in ink with a ballpoint pen. The Center Line can parallel the edge of the platform. Next, draw the Datum Line which must be at ninety degrees to the Center Line precisely, lest the entire hull turns out misshapen.

In establishing the Datum Line, it is tempting to again simply measure from the edge of the platform. Before doing so determine that the platform is absolutely square by first checking that each side of the 2440 mm by 2440 mm section is parallel to and of the same length as its opposing side, then measure kitty-corner across. If both kitty-corner distances measure the same, the platform is square. However, since most sheets of plywood are not truly square, it is likely the platform is also a little off square. If it is off square, the Datum Line could be drawn with a carpenter's square against the Centre-Line, but a far more accurate method is the '3-4-5' formula.

Any right-angled triangle with a hypotenuse (the long side) of five units measures three units along one side of the right angle and four units along the other. The '3-4-5' formula is useful in construction of all kinds.

In this instance apply the formula as follows: measure three units, or a multiple of three, along the straightedge used to mark the Datum Line, measure four units, or the same multiple of four, along the Centre Line, then adjust the straightedge such that the distance between those two points equals five units, or if using a multiple, that multiple of five.

Drawing the Datum Line along the straightedge in that exact position ensures a ninety degree angle to the Centre Line, a hull that is symmetrical, and one less cause for an ailment afflicting most boats, namely, less efficient performance while under sail on one tack than on the other tack.

One additional line, not on the Body Plan, should be drawn. That line needs a name. It could be named "Construction Line" and for the purposes of this book it is so named. This line is parallel to the Datum Line and intersects the Centre Line 200 mm above the point where the Sheer Line[7] intersects the Centre Line. This Construction Line is necessary so that later each of the fifteen frames can be erected on the temporary building frame at their correct height.

Once the grid of the Body Plan has been drawn in ink with ball point, the curved lines of each rib can be drawn using a different colour ink. This requires plotting all the points where each rib line intersects with the grid lines. These points are precisely determined according to the measurements given in the Offset Table. Since this requires nearly four hundred individual measurements it is helpful to hammer a 25 mm finishing nail into the platform at each point where the Centre Line intersects with each line of the grid. Leave about 6 mm of the nail above the deck. Hooking the tape measure behind a thin nail makes accurate plotting so much easier and less open to error. Just don't step on those nails!

Note, all dimensions on the Offset Table are to the very outside of the finished hull and deck, therefore, the thickness of both the hull and deck planking must either be deducted from the relevant dimensions, or once drawn, each rib's line must be duplicated by a parallel line separated by the hull or deck's thickness. Since there will be an abundance of lines already, I prefer the first method. On *Lady Jayne* the hull's planking is 16 mm in thickness and the deck 12 mm. These amounts are deducted from each of the relevant dimensions as given in the Offset Table.

Lofting these lines and deducting the appropriate dimensions all requires great concentration, and even then, mistakes will be made. In addition to your own mistakes, expect occasional errors among the many numbers in the Offset Table. Mistakes and errors will show when the curves of the lines fail to be fair, or when the lines at the various stations show an irregular pattern. If an error in the Offset Table is suspected,

---

7        Sheer Line denotes the line where hull and deck meet.

confirm by scaling that dimension from the Body Plan. Lofting provides an opportunity to see the form of the hull take shape and to anticipate the flow of the keelsom[8], stem[9], and planking from station to station. As these lines are drawn always check for fairness. Fairness of any one rib is increasingly easier to spot the more ribs are plotted and drawn.

A smooth hull with elegant lines is born during lofting

Start with simple frames such as those found at the first three stations. After plotting the points of the ribs that make up the frame at Station One, hammer a 25 mm nail partially in at each of the diagonal grid lines, bend a batten against the nails and secure the batten with nails, or weight blocks, at the Centre and Sheer Lines. Carefully check the curvature for fairness and correspondence to the Body Plan, then draw the line in ink. Do first one side of the Centre Line then the other. You have completed lofting the outline of the frame at Station One. Repeat this process

---

8      Keelsom is the main timber that supports and holds the frames together.

9      Stem is the extension of the keelsom at the bow.

for each of the stations. After all the ribs are drawn the Sheer Line can be drawn. Remember to deduct the thickness of the deck!

The lines should be drawn very distinctly because the platform surface is subject to much work and traffic producing many scuff marks, even with soft-soled shoes. When all stations are complete the exact location of the keelsom can be filled in and drawn. I made the keelsom 100 mm wide by 50 mm thick along its entire length and the stem 75 mm wide. The stem passes through Frame One, hence those ribs stop 37.5 mm short of the Centre Line, all other ribs stop 50 mm from either side of the Centre Line, or, where the keelsom is wider than 100 mm, the ribs may rest on top of the keelsom. In those locations the keelsom needs to be widened with appropriately sized and shaped blocks fastened on either side of the keelsom between the ribs, but that is for much later.

Determine the distance from the Datum Line to the bottom of the keelsom from both the Offset Table and the Construction Plan. To remove all doubt, loft the keelsom profile from the Datum Line down, between Station Three and Station Twelve, inclusive, using yet another colour ink to keep all the lines clearly apart. Lofting this section is also helpful for establishing the height of the gussets that keep the two ribs of each frame securely together and the gussets' bevel where they rest on the keelsom.

The only gussets for which height is critical (since they form stringers for the cockpit sole floor boards) are at Stations Six and Eleven. At all other stations the height of the gusset is judged by how much strength is needed. I cut the gussets from 50 mm thick White or Red Oak stock. The following table shows the height of *Lady Jayne's* gussets above the keelsom at their narrowest side, that is, the bevel and however much the gussets project along side the keelsom, are all in addition to the dimensions shown in this table.

| Station | Minimum gusset height above keelsom, in mm. |
|---|---|
| #1 | 2 |
| #2 | 2 |
| #3 | 3 |
| #4 | 75 |

| | |
|---|---|
| #5 | 75 |
| #6 | 100 |
| #7 | 125 |
| #8 | 228 |
| #9 | 190 |
| #10 | 160 |
| #11 | 70 |
| #12 | 50 |
| #13 | 50 |
| #14 | 50 |

The keelsom and the gussets can now be lofted for each station. To avoid confusion number the gussets appropriately. Also, note that the Station Nine frame rests on a block of 'deadwood', which in turn rests on the keelsom.

Finally, using yet different colours loft the Stem and Stern sections from the offsets shown. It is possible to find some part of the working platform for these sections and the various colours will keep the lines distinct. While you will not work on all of these sections simultaneously, it is important to have them all plotted in actual size, available for checking how one part fits into other parts.

When lofting the Stem, pay particular attention to the amount deducted from the various measurements for the thickness of the hull. As the Stem sweeps upward the amount deducted increases substantially due to the acutely pointed bow. On a scrap piece of plywood, layout, in actual size, the pointed bow of the deck. Take the angles off the Construction Plan with a set-square. Then show the thickness of the hull's planking, both on port and starboard. Measure the distance between the inside and outside of the planking along the deck's center line. Deduct that distance from the measurement that determines the distance from Station One to the finished bow. You'll note it is substantially greater than the 16 mm normal planking thickness.

Look over your lofting and carefully check whether the lines correspond to the plans and flow fairly as they should. Any mistakes here will be costly. Double checking the measurements at this stage is very prudent. Then stand back to see the shape of your boat, it is all there on a few sheets of plywood, imagine the simple, yet strikingly beautiful, lines. Cherish this modest milestone with a deserved sense of accomplishment.

## Band Saw Cutting

The Dragon's unique hull lines are determined by the precise measurements that shape the curvatures at each of the fifteen stations, or cross-sections. *Lady Jayne's* skeleton consists of a frame at each station. Each frame consists of two symmetrical ribs, one for starboard, and one for port. Each rib consists of two strips of white oak that are steamed, bent into shape and then laminated. The strips measure 12 mm by 34 mm each. If I had to do it again, I would make the ribs from three pieces, each 9 mm thick. Three pieces would bend easier and once laminated hold their shape better.

When cutting the stock to size allow for one or two passes through the thickness planer for a smooth surface. However, not all surfaces need to be smooth. I planed the edges and one face. The planed face is for the inside of the hull. The outside face is shaped and added to during the fairing of the frames before the planking can be applied. The in-between surfaces that meet can be left rough sawn, provided it is not too rough. The rough surfaces provide good bonding for the adhesive during lamination. You may consider planing the edges *after* lamination. While I did not do so, I should have. By the time I recognized this omission it was too late, since it would mean removing more stock and reducing the width to less than 34 mm.

Planing the edges after lamination lessens the need to sand the edges. The sanding can be considerable. During steaming the grain lifts and during lamination the edges do not always meet perfectly. Planing the ribs after lamination saves time and makes a cleaner product.

When cutting stock into strips, expect that some strips will break on bending due to knots or short, uneven grain. Also, it takes some experimentation to establish how long your stock needs to be steamed. If it is over-steamed some pieces might turn into noodles and not bend well. For those reasons cut more strips than the number you need.

I used a band saw to cut the strips from rough planks 50 mm thick and 200 mm, 250 mm, and 300 mm wide. Cutting these strips for the ribs was but the beginning of much, much more cutting of hardwood on the band saw. Multiple problems prevented the band saw from running and cutting properly. It took time and much trial and error to correct. First, a band saw needs to be set up and aligned with great care. If the alignment blocks that guide the blade are off, even marginally, the cut face inside the kerf will be jagged instead of smooth, or the blade will burn the wood on one side or the other of the kerf. As long as the cut is not smooth and free of burning, do not be satisfied. Keep adjusting the alignments.

A few more band saw essentials. After warming up the blade will stretch, therefore the tension should be re-checked. Never compress the spring fully and release the tension on the spring when not in use, such as overnight. For blades that are more than 6 mm wide, crowned wheels are not the best. Use a flat wheel. On crowned wheels align the blade just a little forward of centre. Remove sawdust from the wheel tires with steel brush or sandpaper, and occasionally smooth back edge of blade with a file or grindstone. It will tend to develop a small ridge.

In addition to correct alignment, blade type and saw speed are most important. I wasted much time, money and effort learning that the speed on my band saw was too high for hardwoods. I kept experimenting with blades, buying all kinds, fine-toothed, and coarse-toothed, cheap and expensive blades, different tooth shapes, different types of steel, including carbide, and I tried running the blade at different speeds and varied levels of tension, but nothing was satisfactory. Some blades broke, some burned, and often blades gummed up for not clearing the sawdust.

The Thomas Skinner firm, with a location in Richmond, is a specialty dealer in band saw blades for industrial use. Since they deal primarily in blades to cut steel, their personnel, though trying to be helpful, lacked the specialized knowledge this project requires. On the verge of buying a bigger band saw I was rescued by a fellow customer. Hearing my problems while standing at the customer order desk, he said, even though he was but a few years my senior, "Sonny, you are too much in a hurry." He then explained that the speed should be drastically reduced. His sense was that the blade, even at the machine's low speed, turned so fast as to overheat and to then burn instead of cutting the wood fibre.

This free advice proved absolutely correct. By changing the pulley the speed was reduced by half and the cutting improved significantly. Also, I found a hook-type tooth to work best. For cutting hard wood, use blades 18 mm wide, coarse-toothed, three teeth per 25 mm, of carbon flex-back steel. To preserve a blade for cutting long straight boards, do not even think of using the same blade for cutting curves or circles.

## Steaming

Before anything else, plan where and how to place the stock when taken out of the steam box. Bending must be completed very quickly after removal from the steamer. Ensure that all the jigs and clamps are in place, as well as thongs for removing the wood, heavy gloves for handling the stock, and a clear plan for placing the strips in the jig starting from what end. Think about how the pieces will be placed in the steamer, which end should come out first and in what order the pieces will be placed in the box. A dry run, dress rehearsal won't hurt. Have everything prepared in advance, and all tools and clamps laid out in place. Also, remember, steam is hot, it can scald. When opening the end door to remove the stock stand aside till the worst blast of steam has escaped and then work as quickly as possible.

Start the kettle, bring the temperature inside the box to boiling, insert the pieces, in their proper order, and mark the time. The rule of thumb dictates stock should stay in the steamer thirty minutes for each 12 mm of thickness, regardless of width. Deviation from this general rule is due to variation in species of wood, moisture content, and the difference between kiln-dried and air-dried wood.

Through some trial and error I established that the kiln-n-dried White Oak I had bought should be steamed for forty minutes for each 12 mm thickness. Some pieces, perhaps because of a twisting grain or for being sap wood as opposed to heart wood, seemingly over-cooked and bent into uncontrollable, irregular shapes, rather than an even, fair curvature, but for most pieces forty minutes was just about right on.

One note of caution, don't let the kettle run dry. I did and as a result it burned out the element. My steam box can easily go for forty minutes on one kettle without a re-fill of water, but when steaming heavier stock requiring more time the kettle needs to be removed and re-filled before it runs dry. Add to the total time required for steaming the time it takes to bring the temperature inside the box back up.

## Bending

Start with the relatively easy bending of the ribs on the first and last number of stations. First cut the rib blanks or strips to length. Measure the distance along the rib line, starting about 50 mm beyond the keelsom, along the curvature, past the Sheer Line, and add 50 mm beyond the Construction Line. After the frame is assembled the ribs will be cut precisely to fit against the keelsom. At the other end, the ribs can run out randomly past the Construction Line. They will eventually be trimmed at the Sheer Line.

When selecting stock for the ribs and cutting the ribs to length avoid any stock with knots. Knots will not bend into a fair curve. Also avoid, for the same lamination, strips that were adjacent to each other in their original stock. If you cannot avoid that, at least turn every second one end for end. By staggering any weakness or irregularity in the grain the laminated rib will be stronger.

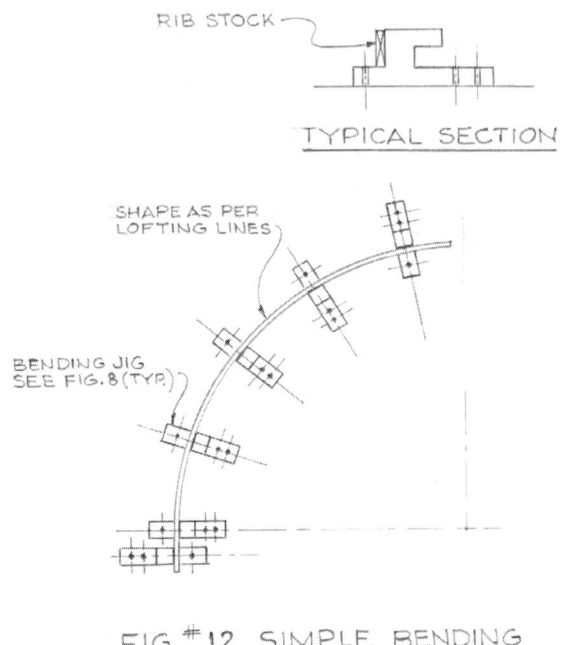

RIB STOCK

TYPICAL SECTION

SHAPE AS PER
LOFTING LINES

BENDING JIG
SEE FIG. 8 (TYP.)

FIG. #12 SIMPLE BENDING

Since these first, simple frames do not require curves with a very sharp radius those ribs can be bent against bending jigs spaced about 250 mm apart along the inside of the curvature (fig. 12). The bending jigs are screwed onto the lofting platform with two screws. Plan to start bending the rib at the end closest to the keelsom. Place one bending jig near that end on the outside of the curvature right on the rib line and another on the opposite side about 50 mm away from the keelsom with just enough space between the two for the rib blanks to fit between the two.

The rib blanks will swell during steaming, therefore make the space between the two jigs a little wider than what is needed while the blanks are still dry.

The last bending jig is placed on the inside of the bend at the Sheer Line. When the rib blanks are taken out of the steamer, place them between the two jigs at the keelsom end, in one swift motion sweep them against the bending jigs, and secure them at the Sheer Line with a clamp.

Additional clamps may be required anywhere along the rib to bring the strips together and snug against the bending jigs. Now place an additional bending jig against the outside, at the Construction Line, such that the temporary 'tail-end' of the rib will fairly follow the curvature of the rib.

The ribs at stations Six through Eleven inclusive, are a little more challenging. Not only do they have a reverse curve but one of those curves has a tight radius. Bending a tight radius stretches the wood fiber on the outside such that it could cause breakage. Fibers on the inside may separate, wrinkling the surface. These potential problems can be largely avoided as follows: on the outside place an additional, surplus strip for the length of the sharp radius, and on the inside use a solid block (fig. 13). The additional, surplus strip might stretch and suffer some breakage on the outside of the bend while offering protection for the blanks that count. As before, cut the rib blanks to length and screw the bending jigs in place starting with the solid block, then one jig opposite the block and perhaps one or two additional jigs on the inside of that first, tight curve near the solid block, but no more. The remaining jigs cannot be screwed down until the rib is bent in place.

Remember to steam one additional, surplus piece. It should be sufficiently long to reach around the solid bending block to the next jig. When the rib blanks come out of the steamer place them, including the short, surplus blank, against the solid block, bend by hand as far as possible, and immediately use clamps to bend the rib all the way against the solid block.

Also clamp the rib against the first jig past the block. Quickly, screw down the remaining jigs on the inside of the second curve. Remember, the outside of the rib must follow the line as drawn on the working platform, hence, these latter jigs must be back from the line a distance equal to the thickness of the rib. In preparation for that, it is useful to make appropriate markings on each side of the bending jigs beforehand. Bend the rib against these jigs, secure with clamps and two more jigs on the outside, one at the Sheer Line, the other at the Construction Line. That is a lot of work to accomplish before the stock cools off. You must either work extremely fast or get help. This is an appropriate time for an extra pair of hands. One remedy is to have a rag in a bucket of hot water. While setting the jigs drape a steaming hot rag over that part of the rib which still needs bending to keep it from cooling off too much.

*Lady Jayne's* Station Eight frame has one additional strip making the thickness of those ribs 38 mm. At Station Eight the beam is at its widest, therefore this frame bears a greater pressure load. After bending a rib leave it overnight in the jig to dry. Next morning, prepare for lamination. If the grain on the in-between surfaces is raised because of the steam, sand with eighty grit sandpaper, brush off the sawdust, and glue up the strips. I used a two-compound, marine glue called UF 109, which has since been pulled from the market in some countries. An appropriate substitute is TiteBond II, but if in doubt, use epoxy. I am not sure epoxy is necessary for this job. Convenience is the biggest advantage of a product such as TiteBond. It needs no mixing, has nearly unlimited pot life, and washes off with water. In my experience, it stands up very well.

Then, before removing all the jigs, remember to make another rib just like it for the other side of the frame.

To speed up production, it is possible to work on more than one rib at a time. In addition, consider preparing the gussets while waiting for the ribs to dry and cure. For the stations near the stem and stern the gussets will fit overtop and beside the keelsom. For stations near the centre of the hull gussets rest on top of the keelsom. In either case, use a bevel square to find the appropriate bevel for each gusset from the lofted lines, or the Construction Plan.

When the gusset is cut with the appropriate width and bevel, shape the ends to conform to the curvature of the ribs by scribing the rib line as lofted on the working platform onto the gusset. Next, cut a rabbet along each end to receive the ribs. The rabbet should be 25 mm deep and as wide as the rib is thick.

Be careful to put the rabbet on the correct side. The bevel of the gusset dictates on which side of the frame the gusset belongs. Read the Construction Plan and note that at Stations One through Eight inclusive, the gusset is forward of the frame, at Stations Nine through Fourteen inclusive, the gusset is aft of the frame.

Now is the time to pre-drill holes for the bolts. Gussets are fastened to the ribs and to the keelsom with 6 mm stainless steel carriage bolts, two at each rib and two through the keelsom, except the Station Eight gusset takes three bolts to fasten to the ribs. Also, gussets at Stations Six through Ten, inclusive, do not need the carriage bolts into the keelsom.

At those stations the gussets are fastened to the keelsom with the 18 mm diameter stainless steel bolts that will carry the lead keel.

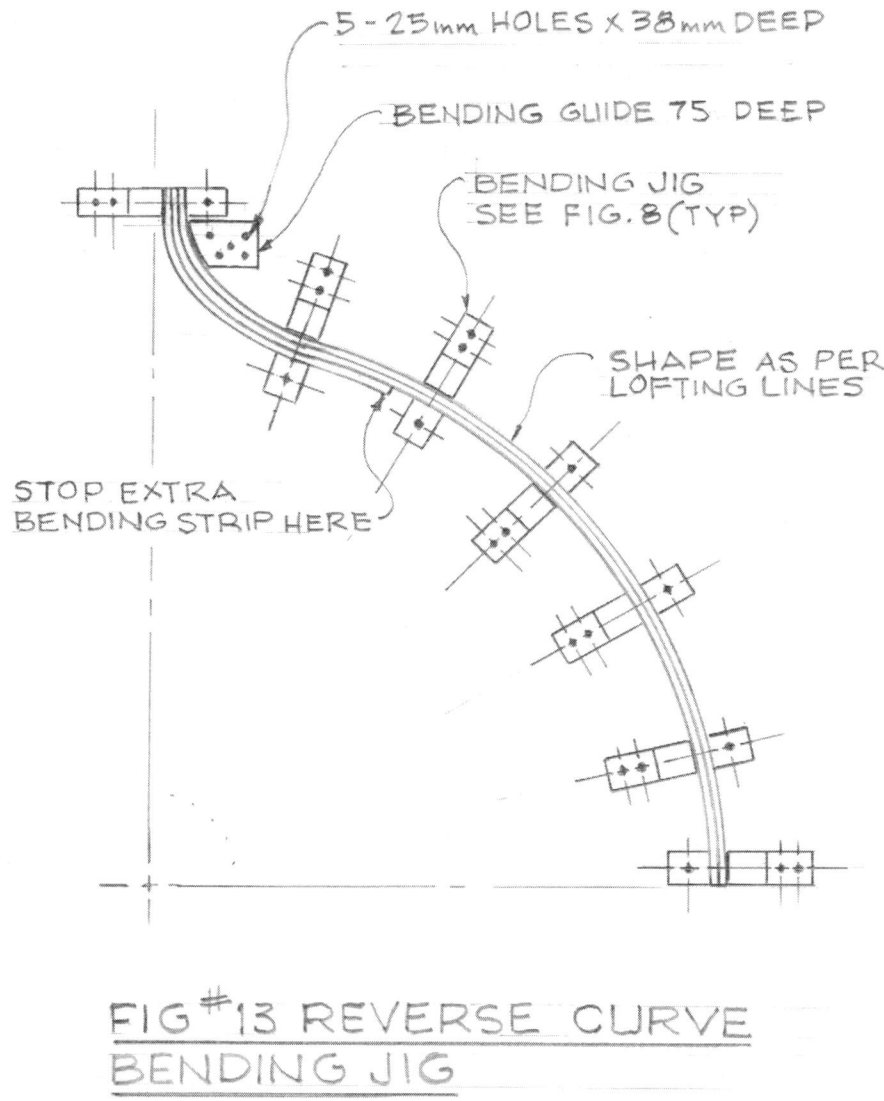

5 - 25mm HOLES x 38mm DEEP

BENDING GUIDE 75 DEEP

BENDING JIG
SEE FIG. 8 (TYP)

SHAPE AS PER
LOFTING LINES

STOP EXTRA
BENDING STRIP HERE

FIG #13 REVERSE CURVE
BENDING JIG

Those big bolts need to be exactly on the Centre Line, except at Station Seven, which has two such big bolts, each centered 56 mm from the Center Line. Before drilling these 18 mm holes provide a countersink on the top side. The diameter and depth of the countersink must be sufficient to receive a washer, lock washer and nut. Similarly, before drilling the 6 mm holes in the gussets for the bolts into the keelsom, countersink for a washer, lock washer, and nut on the top edge of the gussets. Those carriage bolts are driven from below through the keelsom into the gusset.

To my regret, I forgot to provide for drainage openings in the gussets. At this stage it is so simple. At each gusset cut away a corner on both sides of the keelsom, sufficient to leave a channel of no less than 9 mm at what will be the lowest spot inside the hull at that station. If not provided for now, such a drainage channel must be drilled later, a most awkward operation.

When all the ribs are completed they need to be assembled into frames. You will quickly note the springback. The ribs have lost some shape but can be eased back into place by a few strategically placed jigs. Start assembling the frame by fastening the gusset to the ribs using the marks that were transferred before the ribs were removed from the working platform. Clamp the gusset to the ribs and on the drill press complete the bolt holes in the gussets through the ribs. In addition to the bolts, use epoxy, slightly thickened. The forces a hull must withstand are difficult to overestimate. Build strong!

Place the frame on the platform and line up the ribs were they belong with some bending jigs. Prepare a 38 mm by 89 mm as a temporary collar tie holding the frame together at the Construction Line. Since this needs to withstand considerable force secure the 38 mm by 89 mm to the ribs with both glue and wood screws. For the 38 mm by 89 mm, I used old, well-seasoned stock full of bends and twists. The twists matter not, except the 38 mm by 89 mm must touch the point where the Center Line and Construction Line intersect. Both ends should have a rabbet to receive the ribs. If the 38 mm by 89 mm are twisted, as were some of mine, align the inside face of the two rabbets, lest the twist is transferred to the frame.

The gusset, plus the 38 mm by 89 mm at the Construction Line, and a temporary brace between the two will hold the frame together. Use plenty of additional temporary braces to maintain the rib's profile. Those braces will be in place for a long time and do an important job. Don't be stingy, secure the shape of the ribs generously. The uniformity and fairness of the hull depend on it. I used plenty of cut-offs of OSB board scrounged from residential construction sites. They can fan out from the 38 mm by 89 mm and should be fastened with stainless steel screws.

I did not use stainless steel and found ordinary steel wood screws very difficult to extract from the oak ribs several years later when the hull had been turned and all the temporary supports needed to come out.

Also, drive the screws on an angle into the oak ribs such that there is room to extract them. Visualize how the hull curves in relation to the trajectory of an exiting screw. I didn't, and paid for it, dearly. Remnants of a steel screw cannot be left in the hull of a boat without inviting rust and rot. That is an additional reason for using stainless steel screws rather than just steel. If the screw must be left in there is not potential harm.

However be aware that not all stainless steel is of the same quality. It is most frustrating to drive a stainless steel screw and have the head pop off without cause. Because cordless drivers are ever more powerful and oak is, as always, a hardwood, it is as easy as it is mindless to drive a screw such that the head pops. When the countersink and pre-drilling are done carefully and properly and the torque of the cordless adjusted appropriately, heads should not pop. Buy quality and with appropriate care, no heads will pop. The stainless steel designation by itself does not guarantee quality. Know your product and trust your suppliers.

Before removing each frame from the building platform for the last time transfer the following crucial marks from the lofting platform to the frame.

1. Mark the Centre Line both on the gusset and the 38 mm by 89 mm.
2. Also, the 38 mm by 89 mm should touch the Construction Line where it intersects the Centre Line. If not, any deviation should be noted and marked on the 38 mm by 89 mm. The Centre Line mark will position the frames between star board and port, while the Construction Line mark determines the frames' height. Thus the precise shape of the hull's sheer and keel lines are determined.
3. Mark the keelsom on the ribs and after removing the frame from the platform the rib ends can be cut to receive the keelsom.
4. Mark the Sheer Line on the ribs.

Forgetting these markings is not a serious error, but locating the marks is so much easier and more accurate at this stage.

You now have a collection of fifteen frames each of which represents the precise cross section of the hull at a unique point along the hull length. These frames will define the hull shape and give it strength. Each frame is indispensible and no one frame is more important than any other. Together, each in their own place they will make up the hull. The next step is to build a construction platform to temporarily mount the frames in their own unique location holding them in place until the keelsom, sheer batten, and planking will keep them in place permanently.

*CHAPTER FOUR*

# FRAMES AND HULL

"I could watch the motions of a sail forever, they are so rich and full of meaning, I watch the play of its pulse, as if it were my own blood there."
Henry David Thoreau

## Construction Frame

The hull is constructed upside down and during construction the hull's frames are held in place on a construction frame. Since the construction frame will be in place for a considerable period of time and must withstand a lot of stress it needs to be solid, well secured, and not subject to settling. *Lady Jayne's* construction frame was built as follows.

The boat house where the construction took place has a dirt and gravel floor. Landscape ties 82 mm by 114 mm spaced about three metres on centre are dug halfway into the gravel and dirt, tamped down, and secured with a pointed stake or two on each end. Then two, 38 mm by 242 mm, five metres long are overlapped and nailed together to obtain one, nine metres length of strong-back. Make one for each side. These are placed on edge on top of the landscape ties in the shape of the hull about 100 mm inside the deck dimensions thus providing a strong-back along each side.

First, secure the forward end, then at about 1200 mm back, halfway back, and three-quarters back place appropriate lengths of 38 mm by 242 mm between the two strong-backs, bring them together with a come-along, and nail to the landscape ties. A 38 mm by 89 mm plate inside the strong-backs and on top of the ties complete this part of the construction frame (fig. 14). To prevent movement ensure the ties are well supported by gravel and tamped down and use plenty of wood screws to keep it all together.

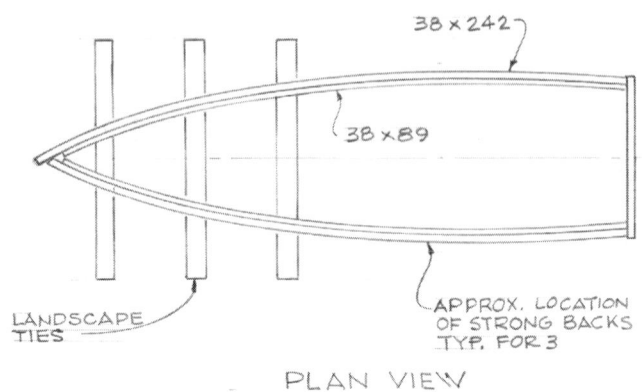

PLAN VIEW

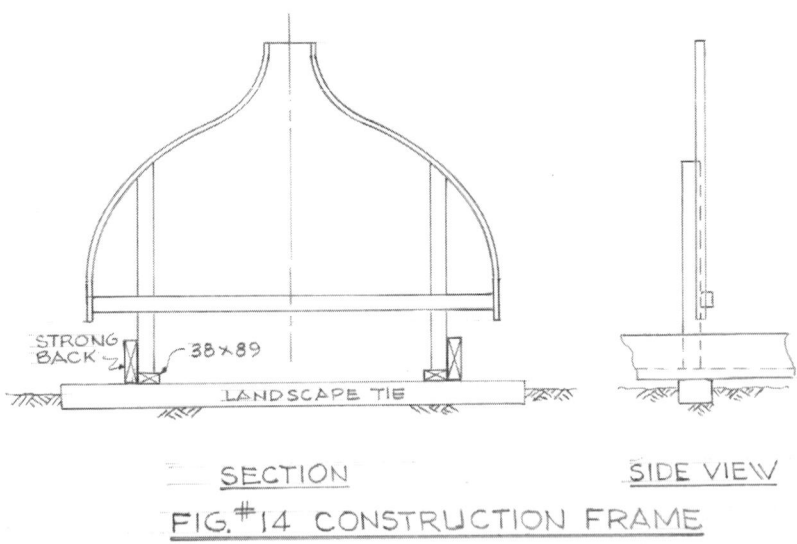

SECTION       SIDE VIEW

FIG.#14 CONSTRUCTION FRAME

To set the frames in place a nylon masonry line is strung down the centre from forward to aft about 300 mm above the strong-backs and later a second masonry line is strung above the first. To mount these masonry lines, erect a well-braced perfectly plumb 38 mm by 89 mm upright from the floor to the rafters at either end about 300 mm beyond the stem and transom. The uprights need to be perfectly plumb in the beam dimension of the hull (fore and aft don't matter). These masonry lines mark the Centre Line of the hull and need to be perfectly level. It is easiest to use a laser level, or as I did, a transit level such as surveyors used before the advent of the laser levels.

Failing either of those, the least expensive and absolutely reliable method is a simple plastic garden hose filled with water. The plastic needs to be sufficiently transparent to see the water level inside when held against a light. If not, insert a short length of clear plastic tubing in both ends. Next, carefully fill the garden hose, avoiding any air locks. Place a thumb firmly on one end and holding both ends together at the same height walk the hose to one end of the construction frame. There attach one end of the hose to the upright and walk to the other end while still holding that thumb firmly in place to not allow air locks to enter the hose.

Air locks in the hose make the level unreliable and must be removed. Attach the hose, remove your thumb, allow the water level to settle, and mark the level at both ends. Use these two levelling marks to fix the masonry line absolutely horizontal and about 300 mm above the strong-backs. Tighten the masonry line till it zings, removing any sway in the middle. You now have a perfectly level and straight line from which to erect the frames.

The height of this line corresponds to the Construction Line you marked on the lofting platform. String a second masonry line above the first to correspond to Water Line 0 by measuring the distance between Water Line 0 and the Construction Line on the lofting platform. The lower masonry line dictates the height of each frame and the higher masonry line is used to measure the profile of the keelsom, and later, the 'dead wood' section of the hull. Both lines determine the position of the frames in the beam (sideways) dimension. What remains is to accurately locate the frames in the fore and aft dimension. For this, fix a batten parallel to the top masonry line about 100 mm off to one side but at the same height. Before erecting this batten mark Stations 1 – 14 plus the stem and transom on the batten.

## Erecting Frames

The frames are supported by two, 38 mm by 89 mm legs that rest on the 38 mm by 89 mm plates. These uprights run alongside the 38 mm by 89 mm collar tie at the Construction Line of each frame and fit underneath the frame's ribs (fig. 14). Start with Frame Eight. From the batten at the higher masonry line drop a plumb line at Station Eight. Draw a line from plate to plate alongside the plumb line and perpendicular to the masonry lines by using the '3-4-5' formula discussed in the Lofting section of Chapter Three. Secure both legs at this line on top of the plate and alongside the strong-back and in a plumb position.

Now, hang the frame against the legs such that the Centre Line marks on the frame, both at the gusset and the 38 mm by 89 mm collar tie, line up with the two masonry lines. In addition, the collar tie needs to just clear the lower masonry line. Now, scribe where the ribs will rest on the supporting legs, remove the frame and cut the legs. Put the frame back into its precise position and secure permanently at the 38 mm by 89 mm collar tie, then ensure the fore/aft position of the frame is plumb and lines up with the Station Eight mark on the top batten, and secure the legs to the ribs.

The remaining frames are similarly placed at their appropriate locations. Keep the frames in place with temporary battens and many braces. Placing the frames in their precise position requires much measuring and use of the level to ensure all relevant lines are perfectly plumb. Also, watch for any twists in the frames and correct such twists with additional bracing. To keep the frames perfectly aligned it helps to place a 100 mm wide batten temporarily on the gussets in the keelsom slot.

Erect frames on a sturdy construction frame

Frequently check that the frames remain plumb in all relevant dimensions. To be off even slightly is to permanently disfigure or misalign the hull. Erecting the frames is a very particular but rewarding task. With each frame the lovely hull shape emerges more fully.

## Keelsom

**N**ext, the 50 mm by 100 mm oak keelsom can be placed and fastened with epoxy and two, 6 mm stainless steel bolts at each gusset. Start with the aft section from the transom to approximately Frame Nine. It is the most difficult section of keelsom since there is some bending centred near Frame Eleven. Both ends can run wild for now to be trimmed more precisely later. Bending solid hardwood in this dimension, even slightly, is a challenge and will require steaming. In addition, before steaming this section, cut two kerfs through the 100 mm dimension, one, one-third from the top and the other, one-third from the bottom, thus creating three equally thick layers of approximately 16 mm each. Do this for approximately 600 mm centered over the required curvature. Start the kerf by drilling a 6 mm hole at one end to insert a coping saw blade. Such a thin blade ensures a minimum of stock is removed.

It is not necessary to steam the entire keelsom length. Remove both ends of the two metre steam box, insert the stock and stuff the ends with rags. Even with steaming and the sawn slots, it will take considerable force to bend. After steaming lay the keelsom in place and pull down near Frame Eleven with a come-along. To not place undue strain on the frames at the two ends, shore up Frames Ten and Fourteen with solid support from the gusset down to the landscape ties and provide extra bracing to keep the frames plumb upright under pressure.

Provide a solid anchor for the come-along by placing a short beam under two landscape ties and chain the come-along to that beam. Obviously, all that should be in place before steaming so that bending can take place with a minimum of delay. When firmly supported it will bend easily under the force of the come-along and as the keelsom settles into the remaining frames it forms a perfect curvature establishing the sweep of the hull from the keel aft. Let dry overnight and next day, remove, force epoxy into the kerfs, apply epoxy at the gussets and ribs, force back into position and insert bolts.

Do not release the come-along until planking up to that spot makes removal necessary. And then, before removing the come-along brace the keelsom at this section to prevent spring-back.

The next section of keelsom runs from the stem to the aft side of the keel. This length may require joining two pieces. A simple butt joint reinforced by a spline is adequate if the joint is well within the section above the keel. If you use a lead keel, and not iron, two additional 50 mm layers of oak stock over the keel section provide for lamination with epoxy and bolts. Again, both ends can run wild for now. This section of the keelsom requires a slight bend near Frame Five. Follow a similar procedure, except it should not require the kerfs; it may or may not require steaming.

## Stem and Transom

The stem section needs to be cut, steamed, bent, and laminated on the lofting platform. It is best to make the laminated strips no thicker than 6 mm. The stem is then fitted against the keelsom with a long scarf joint, apply epoxy and bolts. When placing these bolts, keep in mind that along this section a considerable amount of stock will be removed on the outside of the keelsom and stem during fairing. Countersink the heads of the carriage bolts sufficiently. Also, near Station Two a mounting bracket on the inside of the keelsom for the forestay requires three or four 6 mm bolts. Those bolts can do double duty to also secure the stem to the keelsom.

The transom section is next. *Lady Jayne's* transom was cut from 18 mm plywood and lined on the outside with 5 mm African mahogany. The keelsom is cut and the transom is fixed against the keelsom with a knee, cut from oak. All around the inside of the transom should be reinforced with 18 mm battens to provide more contact surface where the deck and hull meet the transom.

You will discover, as I did too late to my regret, that the acute angles of the hull at this point demand making the initial cut of the transom plywood significantly more acute than the dimensions on the Lofting Platform (except along the deck side).

Plot the dimensions on the plywood remembering that the measurements given are for the finished hull. Cut the plywood leaving ample room for the acute angles particularly along the transom's bottom (which during construction is on top). Mark the Centre and Sheer Lines. Start by fastening the plywood sheet against the keelsom at its appropriate height, level the plywood sheet from side to side, and determine the correct rake, or backward slope, of the transom, then cut a knee to secure the plywood sheet to the keelsom.

## Dead Wood

The keelsom and 'dead wood' sections can now be completed. For the 'deadwood' section use 50 mm stock, prepare pilot holes (see two paragraphs down) and laminate as needed to provide a solid block of wood between Frame Nine and the keelsom. In addition to epoxy, use some 12 mm ready-rod to fasten this piece of 'deadwood' to the keelsom. Similarly, build up the 'deadwood' area fore of the rudder. When placing ready-rod bolts to hold it all together, remember the heavy bolts for the keel are yet to come and will do double duty in that they will both attach the lead keel to the hull and also attach the dead wood to the keelsom.

It is important to take considerable time determining the exact location and rake (angle) of the rudder. Using the two masonry lines as reference points fix temporary battens along the exact leading edge of the rudder. Then cut, install, and fasten the 'deadwood' from the keelsom up to that line. Later during fairing, the 'deadwood' sections need to be shaped with an electric plane, grinder or heavy-duty sander.

With the 'deadwood' in place, drill the holes for the various bolts that run from the frame gussets through the keelsom, and in some instances through the 'deadwood' into the lead keel. Great care should be taken to drill these holes perfectly straight and perpendicular. To that end, where these holes run through the 'deadwood' it is best to prepare the 'dead wood' before assembly with a pilot drill hole. As mentioned above, the 'deadwood' consists of two pieces of oak, 50 mm thick, centered at the Centre Line, laminated and then built up and faired as needed. Before laminating and mounting the 'deadwood' stock in place, run a saw cut about 3 mm deep and the width of the saw's kerf in line with the bolt hole at each Station on the inside face of each piece of 'deadwood'. Preparing these pilot drill holes avoids much grief in accurately placing the bolts into the lead keel mould before pouring. (see Lead Keel section, Chapter Five)

## Lead Keel

*L*ady *Jayne* has two layers of 50 mm oak laminated between the keelsom and the keel. This additional piece of 'deadwood' is shaped like the top 100 mm of the iron keel as shown on the plans.

Lead is a deviation from the plan and came about as follows: an iron keel needs to be poured in a foundry and transported. Both cost plenty. In contrast, a lead keel can be poured by anyone in their own backyard. The lead can be transported in small quantities over time. It saves big dollars.

In my case the foundry's quote for pouring was $2,600. Then how do you transport 2,000 lbs. from south Surrey to the Sunshine Coast? Making the keel from lead, myself, cost no more than $500. Also, while most iron keels will bleed rust over time, lead does not rust. Perhaps best of all, pouring your own keel is great fun.

But lead weighs more than iron and not all lead is of the same purity and therefore of the same weight. *Lady Jayne's* keel is poured from melted down wheel weights and the volume of 1,900 lbs. was roughly determined by extrapolation from melting a small quantity of lead. Later, before actually pouring the keel, a more precise determination was made (See Chapter Five).

But why 1,900 and not the 2,000 lbs required on the plan? Think of a teeter-totter and how a body gains weight the further it moves from the fulcrum point. By increasing the weight and reducing the volume, the centre of the keel's weight moves down, hence, less total weight is required to produce an equal amount of counterweight when the hull heels under the force of wind in the sails. At this point, the calculations showed that reducing the height of the iron keel by 100 mm was sufficiently close to allow a final adjustment when determining the size of the bilge, which is built into the keel.

The bilge is emptied with a hand powered bilge pump using 18 mm diameter plastic hose. To accommodate this hose, drill a 37 mm diameter hole through the keelsom and the 100 mm of oak 'deadwood', precisely where the Centre Line and the lowest point inside the hull intersect.

## Sheer Batten

The oak sheer batten is next. I suggest the dimensions be 100 mm by 12 mm. The batten must be flush with the outermost edge of the ribs which is along the foremost edge for the frames forward of Frame Eight and along the aft edge for frames aft of Frame Eight. Both at the stem and transom, measure from the masonry lines to establish the Sheer Line. With hand saw and chisel provide a rabbet to receive the batten and delight in working with your razor sharp hand tools. To mark the rabbet and account for the curvature of the sheer line lightly clamp the batten against the ribs at the appropriate height, set your scriber at the thickness of the batten, and scribe the ribs on both sides to establish the depth and angle of the rabbet. Before fastening, clamp the batten in place and carefully check if the sheer batten runs fair.

The sheer batten determines the deck line along the sheer and if at any ribs the batten does not run fair it should be corrected now. Any slight deviation, in or out, may seem hardly noticeable now but will be an eyesore once the hull is turned right-side up and the deck boards are put in place.

The sheer batten is fastened with epoxy and one 6 mm carriage bolt for each rib. Except where otherwise noted, always use stainless steel. When fastened against wood, place both a washer and a lock washer under the nut. Put lots of torque on the nut lest hull vibration will ease off the nut.

## Fairing

Each rib, except for those at Frame Eight, needs a final wedge-shaped strip, allowing the planking to rest on the full width of the ribs. With the sheer batten in place the dimensions of this additional lamination can now be determined at each rib. After this additional strip is in place, check if all the lines run fair. Use a variety of battens and straight edges to lie across the frames in all dimensions. Use a crayon to mark the highs and lows. But double check before doing anything. A high or low spot in one dimension may be correct in another dimension. Shave off the high spots and built-up low spots with tapered wedges, or thickened epoxy. On the keelsom and particularly on the stem as it sweeps toward the very pointed bow and the transom, too, there is much stock to be removed and here the electric plane is greatly appreciated. Fairing at this stage pays big dividends later. Fairing is the key to crafting a perfect hull.

## Mast Pulpit

As mentioned, *Lady Jayne's* mast does not penetrate the deck to rest on the keelsom, instead it rests at the deck level and is held in place by a pulpit. The pulpit is installed at this point since its two 'cheeks' must be bolted to the keelsom. That is impossible to do after the planking has been applied. Finding the exact location and more importantly, its correct rake, is crucially important. In this, the drawings are not much help, particularly for determining rake.

'Rake' refers to the angle at which the mast leans aft.[10] All of us are indebted to Dragon sailors who keep experimenting and freely sharing

---

10      The importance of rake is discussed in Erecting Mast section, Chapter Eight.

their findings. Drawing on a wealth of information on the internet[11] helped determine rake.

*Lady Jayne's* rake is determined as follows:
- Mark the position of the front of the mast along the Centre Line of the deck at 820 mm aft of Station Four.
- Mark the deck where the forestay goes through the deck at 1860 mm forward from the front of the mast. This is the maximum allowed under International Dragon Association rules.
- On the aft side of the mast mark the top of the boom's Black Band at 800 mm from the deck, measured perpendicular to the deck.
- Pull the forestay firmly along the mast and mark the top of the Black Band with tape or felt pen.
- Place the forestay at the mark where it is to go through the deck, pull firmly, and measure the distance from the deck to the Black Band mark along the forestay. When that measurement is 1200 mm the mast has attained its correct rake.

Determining rake requires laying out, from the Lofting Platform, the mast and forestay in actual size from the deck to where mast and forestay meet. As mentioned in Chapter Two (Lofting Platform), ideally there is sufficient room beside the lofting platform. Use battens to layout the mast and forestay. You may need to temporarily extend the lofting platform to loft the deck from the mast forward. Otherwise re-loft just those sections of the hull in a different location on the platform. There are by now so many lines on the platform, a few more won't matter. Use different colours ink and do not erase the lofting. There will be occasional use for them.

By following the directions and measurements above, mast rake is determined and once established can be copied to a pattern of lightweight

---

11      One useful site is at http://www.petticrows.co.uk/trim-tips.shtml. There are several other sites with slightly different information. It is best to experiment to find the optimum rake for your boat and the cut and trim of your sails. These also depend on the conditions in which you sail most frequently. While some adjustment after construction is possible, it is best to get rake as close as possible during construction.

plywood or core board of about one metre for each leg of the angle. Establish the correct rake of the pulpit by lining up the pattern with either of the masonry lines. Remember, everything is upside down. It is a complication that can easily be overlooked but fortunately, such mistakes always come to light quickly. Keep the pattern for later use.

The pulpit (fig.15 a&b) should be nearly fully constructed before installing. Although fittings such as the winch and rope clutches can be installed later, the mounting bases for those fittings should be in place. *Lady Jayne's* pulpit dimensions are somewhat arbitrary, but have worked well. All the wood is Red Oak, except for the two sheaves, which are made from Purple Heart. Two halyards, one for each sail, come down the inside of the mast, down the pulpit, through the rope clutches, over the sheaves, and from there to the winch.[12] The sheaves have a brass bushing which turns on a 12 mm stainless steel shaft.[13] To prevent the sheaves wandering laterally, place a washer on either side held in place with a sleeve cut from brass bushing material. Place such sleeves around the shaft on either side between the washer and pulpit 'cheek'.

The inside of the 'cheeks' have a spline, 9 mm thick, near the top, because oak, while very strong, sometimes tends to split easily, particularly near a butt end exposed to the weather.

When selecting stock for the 'cheeks' check very carefully for any tiny splits that could develop into serious trouble later. The spline on each side is covered with a 3 mm strip of leather. Similar strips of leather are glued to the inside of the cheeks further down at deck level. This leather will hold the mast snugly in place without chafing the wood surfaces. The dimensions for this bottom section of the mast are 80 mm by 89 mm. The pulpit is fastened to the keelsom with epoxy and two 6 mm carriage bolts or threaded rod with washers and nuts.

---

12      For a fuller description of sheaves, see Blocks section, Chapter Seven.

13      Nearly all such materials can be bought secondhand for scrap metal value. I bought much of this at ABC Traders, Richmond, BC.

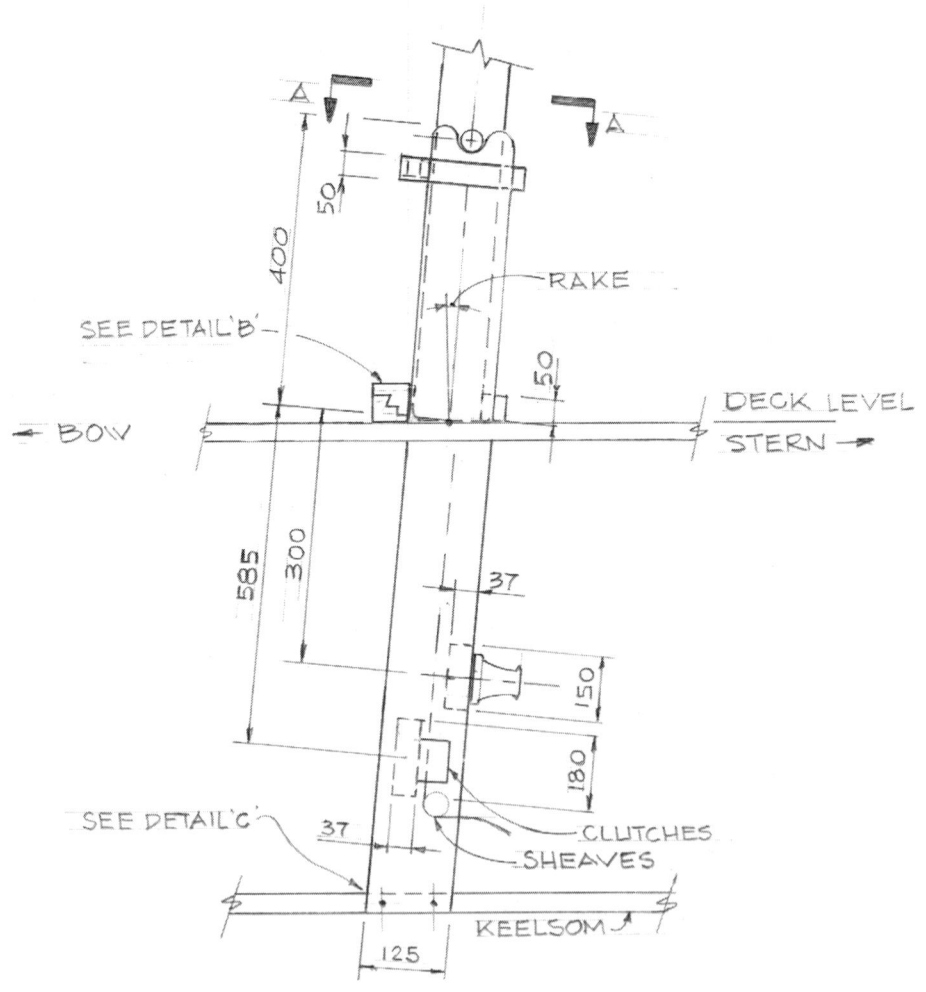

FIG. 15A   PULPIT

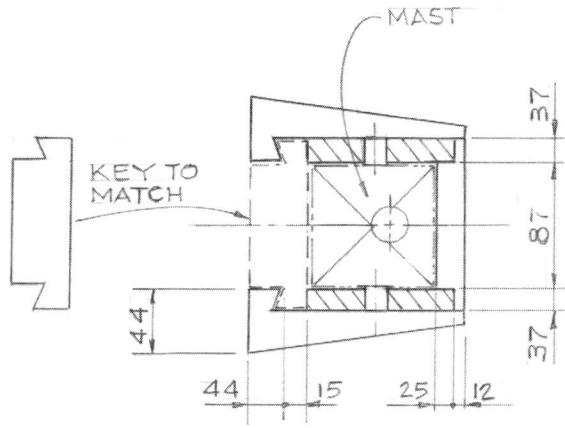

MAST

KEY TO MATCH

37

87

44

37

44 15 25 12

<u>SECTION AA</u> (FIG.15A)

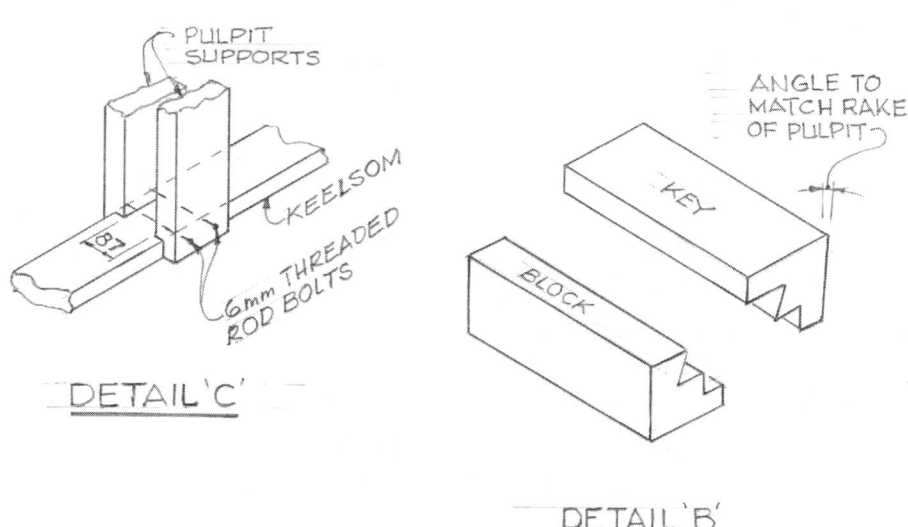

PULPIT SUPPORTS

KEELSOM

87

6mm THREADED ROD BOLTS

<u>DETAIL 'C'</u>

ANGLE TO MATCH RAKE OF PULPIT

KEY

BLOCK

<u>DETAIL 'B'</u>

<u>FIG.#15 B  PULPIT DETAILS</u>

## Mounting Blocks for Engine, Bearings and Stuffing Box

The Dragon design, with a modified cockpit, offers limited but just enough space for an in-board engine and *Lady Jayne* is equipped with a 5 hp, Honda, air-cooled engine. It provides power for limited use and has served me well. However, the decision to install an air-cooled engine in a wooden boat is not universally recommended. Insurance companies take a dim view and if they provide insurance at all, such insurance will not cover fires caused by an air-cooled engine. Special care must be taken to ensure a safe exhaust system and the engine cannot be enclosed but must be exposed to open air while in use.

I have had more advice, and more contradictory advice, about the engine than any other aspect of this project. Originally, I followed the suggestion that the take-off from the engine to the drive shaft would be straight out back from the engine's drive shaft and built a mounting block accordingly. I even drilled a hole through the hull for the drive shaft and installed the stuffing box on a mounting block in front of the through-hull shaft opening.

Then I was persuaded by others who suggested that the engine's drive shaft bearing was designed to take a lateral load but not for a load pushing into the engine. If so, my proposed design would burn out the bearing in no time. Following this latter advice, the engine is mounted just aft of Station Eleven on the port side of the keelsom. The take-off is by v-belt over a 100 mm diameter pulley to a second 100 mm pulley mounted on an 18 mm diameter shaft, supported by two bearings mounted on a mounting block placed on the starboard side of the keelsom. The propeller shaft is linked to the pulley driven shaft by a universal joint. The universal joint is necessary to make the transition from the pulley driven shaft, which is positioned level, to the propeller shaft, which angles down at approximately twenty degrees. The propeller shaft penetrates the hull just forward of Station Twelve. For more detail see Engine and Through-hull Fittings section, Chapter Six (fig.20).

At this stage of the construction it is necessary to shape and install the mounting blocks for the engine, the two bearings, and the stuffing box. To do so requires having these items at hand.[14]

*Lady Jayne's* propeller is a simple, rigid two blades, 200 mm in total length. I considered a propeller with folding blades to reduce drag when not in use. However, the drag would hardly be less on such a small propeller since the hub of a folding propeller has much more bulk, and also the cost is excessive.

All three mounting blocks are made of Red Oak. The engine and the bearings should be at the level position when the boat is resting on its water line. The stuffing box needs to be aligned with the propeller shaft angle. Determine the propeller shaft angle such that there will be at least 75 mm of water above the propeller blade when the boat is stationary. Proper depth will require a universal joint just aft of the shaft bearings. To lower the propeller shaft as much as possible, the pulley on the shaft runs through a slot, cut into that mounting block. To prevent standing water collecting there drill a small draining hole out to the side.

All four mounts (engine, stuffing box, and two bearings) require studs to come up out of the wood to which the fixtures can be attached. These studs are 9 mm or 12 mm threaded rod mounted into the wood with nuts, washers, lock washers and epoxy. Particularly on the engine mount, the studs must withstand considerable vibration. To reduce overall vibration, plan to insert 9 mm rubber between the engine and its wooden mounting block. Do the same for the bearings mounting block. Make the protruding studs sufficiently long to accommodate these rubber cushions. The mounting blocks should be bolted to adjoining frames and keelsom. Later, when planking the hull, ensure plenty of epoxy will further fasten these important mounting blocks to the hull.

---

14      I bought items such as shafts, propeller, and stuffing box at second hand stores, in particular Mariner's X Change in Steveston, BC and Popeye's Exchange in North Vancouver, BC.

## Fittings for the Stays and Shrouds

The forestay, backstay, running back stays, lower and upper shrouds all require fittings where they can be attached to the hull. It is these stays and shrouds that keep the entire rig upright. In a strong, gusty wind and rough seas the stress on them is enormous and breathtaking. It has to be experienced before it is believed. Make these fittings as strong as possible. Over building is almost impossible at this stage.

The exact position where the forestay enters the deck is described above on p.76 in the Mast Pulpit section. Locate that position on the hull with temporary battens and from there use the mast's rake pattern to mark the forestay's location on the stem.

The fore and aft location of the shrouds for the upper and lower spreaders can be scaled from the Sails and Rigging Plan. Sideways they penetrate the deck 700 mm from the Centre Line. With battens mark the precise location where these shrouds enter at the deck and at what angle, both fore and aft and sideways, relative to the mast. Having located where they enter at the deck and at what angle helps determine the exact location where the shrouds attach to the inside of the hull. Remember to think upside-down.

For both starboard and port fashion a mounting beam of approximately 100 mm by 100 mm that will attach between the ribs at Station Six and Five (see picture). Each mounting beam will have two u-bolts of at least 6 mm stainless steel to attach the turnbuckles for the stays. For additional strength install between the u-bolts an upright, of 18 mm stock, from the mounting block to the underside of the deck and sheer batten. The exact location is 92 mm forward of Station Six. That will allow the last deck beam before the cuddy roof to be fastened aft of the upright.

The location of the backstay and the two running backstays is somewhat arbitrary but common sense suggests the further back, the more effective.[15] On the *Lady Jayne* the backstay enters the deck 500 mm from

---

15      However, the further back the running backstays are placed, the more difficult to reach them should there ever be need to replace these blocks or do any maintenance on them. Locating them 800 mm forward of the transom does make repairs possible.

the transom and the running backstays 550 mm from the transom, the latter are 75 mm from the sheer. All three need a steel block immediately below the deck. The backstay runs from that block to a second block fastened to the keelsom.[16] An attachment for that block should be installed now and secured to the keelsom with three or four 6 mm bolts.

Mounting beams for fastening shrouds can't be strong enough

The blocks for the running backstays should also be installed now because they need to be bolted through the sheer batten before any planking is applied. Shape and place a mounting wedge between the sheer batten and blocks to align them properly. In addition, the running backstays require a double block tackle system. One set of double blocks are fastened against the sheer batten near Station Eight and should be installed before applying the hull planking. (See the Rigging Blocks section in Chapter Six)

16      The backstay steel wire attaches to a single sheave block. A rope attached to that single block runs from there over another single block attached to the aft side of the coaming and exits through a cam cleat also fixed to the aft side of the coaming.

You have reached another important milestone. All the various pieces are now in their assigned place and together contribute to something greater than the sum of the parts – a hull *so beautifully proportional that it never fails to turn admiring heads.*

CHAPTER FIVE

# PLANKING, COLOUR SCHEME, TURNING HULL, LEAD KEEL

"I don't like work – no man does – but I like what
is in work – the chance to find yourself."
Joseph Conrad

Long before completing the hull's frame, an order for planking materials needs to be placed. If the choice is mahogany, you must go for the best, which is African Mahogany. Mahogany from the Philippines is soft, lightweight, and lacks a distinguishing grain and deep colour. South American mahogany is better quality, but it too, lacks the strength, density, strong straight grain, and deep colour of African Mahogany.

Vancouver's P.J. White Hardwoods allows you, for a modest premium, to pick over a newly arrived shipment. Getting top grade stock is important and worth the effort and money. Even at top price, the cost of this material is a fraction of the cost of the total project. Look for straight planks with an even and consistent grain. Avoid planks that are bowed, warped or twisted, of course, but also avoid those that are cupped across their width and those wholly, or what is more common, partially cut from either the soft wood near the bark or the obstinate and hard grain from the heart of the tree. In one shipment consisting of two slings I found sufficient planks for *Lady Jayne*, all of great quality measuring 50 mm thick, 4880 mm long and in width varying from 200 mm to 300 mm.

*Lady Jayne's* hull is cold-molded, using epoxy to laminate four layers of thin planking across the ribs and frame. The outer and inner layers consist of African Mahogany cut into strips measuring 5 mm by 75 mm. The two, core layers are rotary mahogany plywood 3 mm thick, cut into strips 75 mm wide and 2440 mm long. The core is basically a filler. There is no need for quality plywood and low quality plywood weighs less.

If I could do it again, I would reduce the thickness of the outer layer from 5 mm to 3 mm and to keep the total hull thickness, increase the thickness of the inner layer from 5 mm to 7 mm.

The slightly thicker inside plank would give more body particularly during the application of the first and second layers. With the ribs 600 mm on centre it is a challenge to keep these first strips together and avoid dips and humps in the wrong places. Also, for the inner layer's surface I planed a small V-joint on each plank to enhance the inside appearance. A 7 mm thickness provides considerable more firmness between the ribs and more material along the edge for laminating adjoining planks than the 5 mm thickness.

While the proposed change in thickness has a solid benefit for the inner layer, the real payoff and primary reason for the suggested change concerns improved durability for the outer layer. A thinner outer layer will withstand sun and weather better than a thicker layer. It is counter intuitive, but true. I know from experience. Having to re-do some of the work concentrates the mind, wonderfully.

Reducing the thickness of the outer layer lessens the ability of strong heat from the sun to lift the plank. A thicker plank retains enough strength to pull away by overcoming the adhesion power of epoxy. Epoxy softens under intense heat, potentially causing the outer planks to lift away from the inner core. To appreciate how much heat can be generated by a summer sun on a dark mahogany surface, place your hand on the surface after a few hours of exposure to direct sun light. The thinner the material the weaker its ability to overcome the adhesive power of epoxy!

For *Lady Jayne's* hull I milled 686 m of 5 mm by 75 mm boards. It is more than required but it allows sufficient choice to select the very best and the remainder is useful for smaller jobs. Cutting that much stock in that dimension is almost too much for the 14 inch band saw, but if the type of blade suits the material and is set correctly, feeding it through slowly will get the job done.[17]

---

17      See Band Saw Cutting section, Chapter 3, for important information about type of blade and cutting speed.

Start by cutting the material into boards about 78 mm wide, sufficiently wide to plane it down to precisely 75 mm. Single-handedly sawing stock 50 mm thick, up to 300 mm wide and 4880 mm long requires at least three portable, standing rollers, one to feed the saw and two to take the stock as it exits the saw. The rollers must be set perfectly and braced to prevent any movement, particularly sideways.

Before cutting the 78 mm wide stock into thin planks plane the edges on a thickness planer to 75 mm width. The thin planks themselves are also planed but only one surface, for both the inside of the hull, and of course especially, the outside. The in-between surfaces can be left somewhat rough, thus giving the epoxy better adhesion.

When sawing the thin planks there are several things to look for with each set of two planks cut. First, you'll want to book-match the planks particularly for the always visible outside of the hull. Lay the two planks, open face, side by side, such that the same saw kerf separates the two open faces and pencil a line diagonally across both faces. Do this on the surfaces that will not require planing. This mark will help recall how the boards relate to each other should there be a mix up. Second, check for any splits, knots, ugly or difficult grain, and other imperfections. Such boards are colour coded with a crayon on the end grain at one end as being third-rate. The absolute best boards in terms of structural soundness and interesting grain pattern are given a different colour indicating they are the very best. All other boards are colour coded as second best.

Note that placing the book-matched sets adjacent to each other in the order in which they came from the stock will not necessarily yield the most interesting pattern. It might be too even in colour and grain, too similar, too bland. It is sufficient that each set of two planks is book-matched. Randomly mixing their origin will make for a more interesting pattern on the hull.

When storing the sawn and planed planks ensure they are placed straight and solid in both directions to prevent warping. Also the place of storage must be of low moisture content. Moisture content is very important, since a moisture content other than very low will allow shrinkage after the planks have been fitted and applied to the hull and possibly opening the joints between the planks.

To apply the planking, start from the sheer line and work up toward the keel. The first two planks can be left their full width for nearly the length of the hull. They require some tapering at the stem. After that each succeeding plank must be tapered significantly, especially toward the stem. The hull's beam is widest at Station Eight, therefore the planks can be their full width at Station Eight. Do not force the planks into any twist.

Forcing the planks creates high and low spots between the ribs increasing the need for fairing. Let the boards find their own natural resting place along the hull shape and taper the edges accordingly. Mark the taper from the underside, then cut the taper a little wide off the pencil mark and complete the trim with a hand plane to make a perfect joint. Planing these long tapers on such thin stock is best done by placing the stock against the front of the work bench in the retractable brackets.[18] For this work use a long hand plane and under-cut the edges to account for the hull's curvature. Apply planks to ribs with epoxy and some counter-sunk, 18 mm stainless steel, flathead screws.

A simple but well-appointed work bench is a delight

To follow the curvature of the hull the beam dimension requires sections of some planks to be steam bended before they can be applied. This is particularly true at the transom, the chine sections and where the hull flows into the keel. To get the planks to 'cup' appropriately at these critical

18      See (fig. 1), Chapter Two.

places, cut a supply of patterns consisting of blocks 37 mm thick and 75 mm in length with a radius along one edge. For each block with a concave radius cut a matching block with a convex radius. The radius should be a little sharper than required by the hull shape to allow for spring-back. After steaming, clamp the plank between these bending patterns, placed at about 150 mm intervals. Dry overnight, then apply the plank to the ribs. Place these bending patterns such that they do not interfere with the ribs and leave them in place on the plank when applied to the ribs until the next plank is applied and the clamps must be removed.

As with so much of wooden boat building, planking the hull is a tedious job that cannot be rushed. The task needs to be done one plank at the time with sufficient time for clamping to allow the epoxy to cure before moving on to the next plank. Fortunately there are two sides as well as fore and aft to allow drying time for the planks while fitting and preparing the next at a different location on the hull.

With every set of two, book-matched planks check if the plank is high or low between the ribs and correct such deficiencies with a temporary support fastened between the ribs to bring the planks up or down as needed. This too, saves much fairing work later. With each successive layer the hull's strength and firmness increases, making the hull's surface more fair. Nevertheless, between layers two and three and again between layers three and four there is a need to fair the surface by filling in the low spots with a mixture of epoxy thickened with micro balloons, or as I did, mixed with fine sawdust. As for the high spots, they need to be sanded down with a disc grinder.

The hull's fairness is determined with a slat, or batten, that is straight and with perfect grain. Bend it across the surface in all directions and mark the low and high spots with two separate colours of crayons. It is important to move the slat across all dimensions before concluding that a particular spot is high or low. What may seem high or low in one dimension could vary when checked in a different dimension.

This job of fairing, too, cannot be rushed and when done accurately will show to great advantage, but not until the final coat of varnish has been applied. That final coat gives the outer layer its permanent high gloss, mirror-like shine. It is only then that imperfections show - when it is too late and nothing can be done about it. You will want the final product to be perfect. That perfection starts when laminating and setting the frames and continues with applying each layer of the hull's planking as accurately as possible.

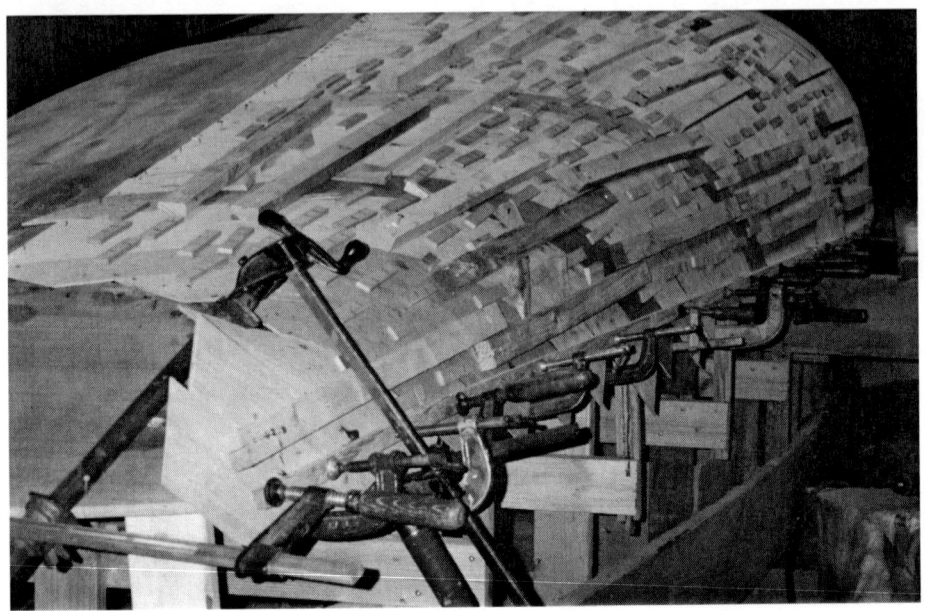

Inner core diagonal planking

The two inner core, 3 mm layers are placed diagonally at about forty five degrees first in one direction with the next layer crossing over in the other direction. This yields maximum strength. Start somewhere amidship around Station Eight. From there, work towards fore and aft. These thin plywood strips can be forced down and held in place with battens, 18 mm by 37 mm of various length laid across the strips and then temporarily fastened against the ribs with wood screws. In addition to these, for the spaces in between the ribs, use 12 mm staples shot through 5 mm thick temporary stock cut out of very soft wood such as Western Red Cedar.

Because the hull's surface curves in all directions make and use a large supply of thin wedges cut from hardwood. Drive these wedges wherever needed between the battens and the planking strip being worked on. A large supply of such wedges in a variety of thicknesses, angles, and sizes is indispensable. Throughout the construction process you will need plenty of them in all kinds of situations.

Do not be stingy with the epoxy or the staples. *Lady Jayne*'s construction consumed 5,000, 12 mm staples for this purpose. Do not leave any air pockets between the layers, be they ever so slight. Water will find its way into those spaces starting rot where you can't see it, nor get to it. Also be sure to fill with epoxy all screw holes left from the temporary battens used to force the planks into place. Similarly, fully fill all staple holes when applying the next layer.

Before applying the fourth and final layer, install a standpipe for the 25 mm stainless steel rudder shaft. The standpipe itself should also be stainless steel, have an inside diameter no less than 32 mm, and have a flange welded to one end. The flange rests on layer three and is fastened with epoxy and some flathead screws. Let the pipe project 5 mm through the flange to make it even with the finished hull surface. The correct angle is established by extrapolating the angle of the aft side of the keel. The length needs to terminate about 100 mm below the underside of the deck. For now, the end can run wild for final trimming later.

The final outer layer of planking deserves the greatest attention. Start at the Sheer Line and work up. Cut the plywood layers along the sheer batten and plane to a very smooth and fair surface. Remember to lower the first hull plank sufficiently so it will cover the 6 mm marine plywood decking. Leave a little extra to be planed smooth after the deck plywood is in place. After the first, outer layer plank has been applied the sheer batten and the three layers applied so far cannot be planed for fairness, or only with great difficulty. Hence, take extra care to get that line absolutely fair. It will always be very visible and noticeable afterwards. Because you are working upside down it is not easy to do, but it is worth doing at this stage.

When tapering the planks, remove wood from both sides of each two-plank, book-matched set. Leave the centre joint intact, thus preserving the book-matched grain as much as possible. Again, let the wood flow naturally along the curvature of the hull starting amid ship and working toward fore and aft. Pressing these planks into place firmly is the most challenging of all. I used lengths of 37 mm by 37 mm stock about one metre long fastened to the ribs above and parallel to the plank being worked on. From these, run battens 18 mm by 37 mm, spaced about 150 mm on centre, down across the plank being worked on and then clamped at the Sheer Line. Thus these battens will follow the curvature of the hull and press the plank being worked on firmly against the layer below. Again, use wedges under the battens wherever necessary to ensure the plank is firmly forced down against the previous layer. Once you have crossed the Water Line you are free to use 12 mm flathead screws anywhere and longer screws where the ribs are.

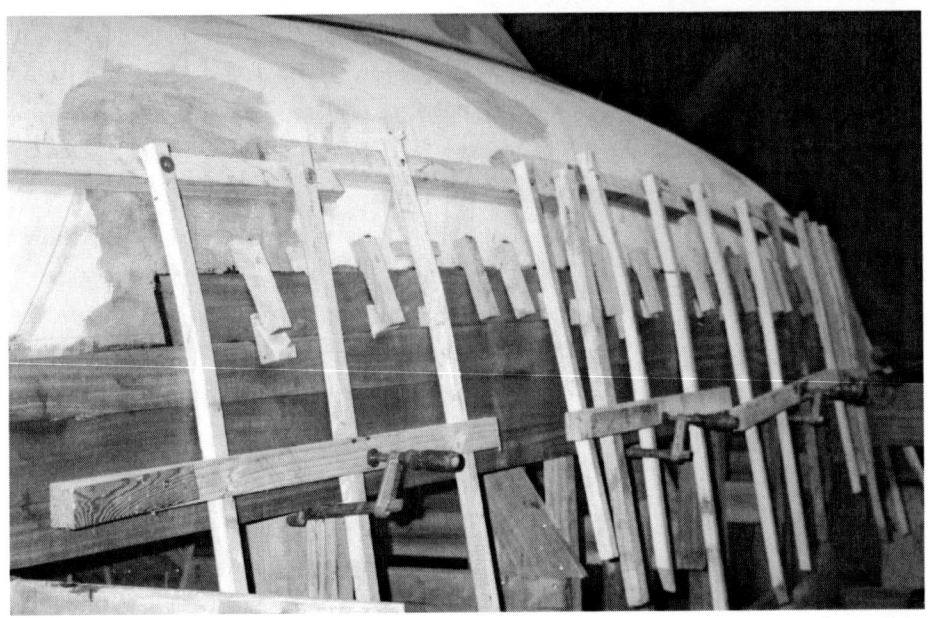

Battens force outer layer of planking to follow hull curvature.
Notice final fairing patches on second inner core layer.

With the hull fully planked what remains is to line the transom also with mahogany. The boards could be run horizontally but I chose to have them fan out from the centre line at 45 degrees, both sides. It makes for an interesting pattern. Next is the stem, requiring solid mahogany from the bow point sweeping down to almost Station Two. First, shape by plane, preferably an electric plane, a flat area about 37 mm at the bow point to about 58 mm wide where it runs out against the keelsom near

Station Two. Against the flat area bend four layers of mahogany stock, each layer 9 mm thick and 62 mm wide. Fasten this in place with epoxy after steam bending to attain the striking sweep of the stem shape. Then trim from both sides with an electric plane to attain a knife edge sharp point along the length of the stem. The four layers of stock should be cut from one piece and kept in their original position. It will minimize the glue line, giving the final laminated product the appearance of one solid piece of mahogany.

Such a finished stem is truly the finishing touch, accentuating the slim, sharp, compelling lines of the Dragon. Do not even think of spoiling this with an ugly, stainless steel eye-bolt for towing.

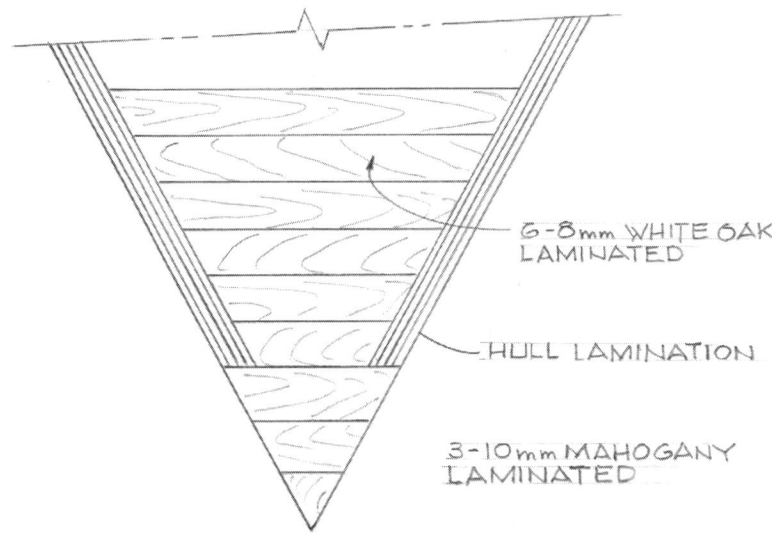

6-8 mm WHITE OAK LAMINATED

HULL LAMINATION

3-10 mm MAHOGANY LAMINATED

FIG. #16 KNIFE-SHARP BOW STEM

Now comes hours and hours of smoothing the hull. I did this mostly by hand. The bulk removal of material might be done by plane, a steel edge, or chards of glass, the latter is my preference. For this collect a bucket of discarded chards at a glass shop. Then sand and sand, finishing with increasingly higher grit sandpaper. To ensure a perfect rounding of the hull's curved surface make a sanding block about one metre long, 75 mm wide out of 3 mm thick plywood with a firm handle on each end. Glue on the sandpaper. To work it, push down hard, while pulling it back and forth diagonally across the planks along the outside curvature of the hull. The same sanding block may be used later for sanding the successive coats of epoxy and varnish.

## Colour Scheme, Staining and Fibreglass.

You may wish to keep the mahogany bright and natural, however *Lady Jayne's* mahogany while kept bright is stained a wonderful deep red wine colour. It brings out the rich wood grain and always draws compliments. Before deciding the hull's colour, consider the entire colour scheme including deck, mast and boom, sails and the inside of the cockpit such as the seats and sole.

*Lady Jayne's* dark reddish hull is complemented by a very deep green (bordering on black) for the cockpit coaming, waterline and dragon ornament (these being the only painted surfaces)[19] The deck is finished with Yellow Cedar strips 6 mm by 37 mm separated by 6 mm wide joints filled with black epoxy and further offset by the red mahogany sheer boards and fish-tail king board down the centre line. Sitka Spruce for mast and boom, both are bright and natural with mahogany spreaders. Her sails are white. Brown sails are more suitable for fishing and freight boats and seem inappropriate for the Dragon lines, since those lines are designed to heighten the appearance of speed. *Lady Jayne's* colour scheme is pleasing and arresting.

Great care should be taken to select appropriate colours. The first thing people see is not the quality of craftsmanship, the variety of exotic woods, or even the pleasing lines, it is colour. It may not seem fair,

---

19      See Coaming and Deck Beams section, Chapter Six for more precise instructions about paint.

but your project will be judged first and foremost by the quality of its colour scheme.

Epoxy will not hold on painted or stained surfaces, except on a water-based stain. Such stains are not common but Mohawk Stains has a good selection of water-based stains. All *Lady Jayne's* mahogany that is easily visible, from the water line up, including the cockpit sole and the beautiful wooden blocks, is stained with Mohawk's transparent Ultra Penetrating Stain, colour: Oxblood #520-24576.

After staining the hull, the Water Line must be established. Ensure the hull is perfectly level in both dimensions on its construction frame, then the Water Line can be established using a laser level, a transit level, or plastic water hose as discussed in Chapter Four. Alternatively, the Water Line can also be marked up from the Construction Line at each station on both sides. A simple method is to tack an upright slat, of appropriate length measured from the Construction Plans, against the end of the 38 mm by 89 mm temporary collar tie holding the frames together at the Construction Line. Mark the hull at regular intervals at this height by placing an ordinary hand- held level from the top of the slat to the hull.

Fibreglass can now be applied from the top of the Water Line to the keel. Do not forget to fibreglass the flat area of oak dead wood where the lead keel will attach, and in particular, line the inside of the hole that will accommodate the bilge hose. Oak is strong but its greatest drawback is that is rots easily when kept moist. The areas where the lead keel attaches to the frame and hull need to be sealed perfectly lest rot sets in where it is most difficult to detect and correct.

*Lady Jayne's* below water surface is fibre glassed using six-ounce cloth and System Three's Silvertip laminating resin. Against the bare wood, stretch out the cloth and hold in place with masking tape, then liberally coat with resin applied with a small, 67 mm wide, throw-away roller. Start applying resin near the centre of the cloth and work towards the edges. After sanding apply one additional coat of resin.

You will spend much time sanding fibreglass and especially epoxy. This is almost impossible to overstate. When you think you are almost done you are probably approaching halfway.

Fibreglass and epoxy tends to clog almost all types of sandpaper. It is essential to purchase product that cuts and remains unclogged. After

experimenting with most sandpaper known to mankind, my recommen-
dation is to invest heavily in both #120 grit 3M (216U) Production RN, Paper
A wt. Open Coat, Free-Cut and #220 grit 3M (415U) TRI-M-ITE FRE-CUT,
Paper A wt, Open Coat. In my experience, on epoxy these 3M products
out-perform all others.

Keep a brush handy to regularly sweep the sandpaper grit clean.
When sandpaper clogs it is useless very quickly.

## The Lead Keel

Constructing the lead keel is one of the most interesting and satisfying
parts of this project. In brief, *Lady Jayne's* 1,900 lbs. lead keel was poured
by melting used wheel balancing weights over an open fire. Follow
these steps:

- Make a male plug out of Styrofoam. Coat
  it with drywall filler and paint.
- Dig a hole in the ground and pour 75 mm
  of concrete around the plug.
- Chip the plug out and pour the lead in.
- Three easy steps. Now for the details.

## Patterns to shape the form of lead keel

From the Keel Plan mark and cut out a series of patterns using 12 mm plywood. The patterns trace the outline of the lead keel at intervals much like the frames outline the hull's shape. The patterns are mounted in their precise location on a plywood platform, and held upright at their correct angle with some bracing slats (see picture). A block of styrofoam is shaped to fit inside these patterns. Styrofoam can be roughly cut with a handsaw. The entire surface is then repeatedly coated with ordinary drywall filler, fitted into the patterns, shaped some more, and finally sanded down to perfect fairness, and a very smooth surface.

After the filler is cured apply three coats of paint. The result is a plug in the exact shape of the lead keel. With subfloor adhesive, commonly used in residential construction, attach the plug's flat side to a chunk of plywood so the plug can be held in place over the hole dug into the ground.[20] In addition, along the flat, aft side where the rudder attaches to the keel, glue a 38 mm by 89 mm. It can run wild a little beyond the keel's bottom edge, this bottom protrusion and a few randomly placed screws sunk partially into the aft side of the 38 mm by 89 mm will hold it in the concrete after the plug is chipped out.

Finally, plan to attach the 'shoe' that holds the bottom end of the rudder shaft. This 'shoe' must be removable from the keel in the event the rudder and shaft need to be extracted from the shaft's standpipe. Two, 6 mm bolts should be fastened through the 38 mm by 89 mm such that each bolt will leave a threaded hole into the lead keel for later fastening the 'shoe' that holds the rudder shaft (fig. 17). In addition to holding the bolts in place, the 38 mm by 89 mm also serves as a nailing platform. Once the concrete has set and the styro foam male plug is removed, a half-round for the rudder's leading edge and a key for the 'shoe' can both be nailed

---

20      It is not easy to keep the styrofoam plug perfectly straight. The force of the concrete can easily twist the plug. The aft end is kept firmly in place but the fore end needs reinforcing. At the Centre Line near the fore end drill a 25 mm hole through the plywood and through the styrofoam plug and insert a dowel. Let the dowel extend above the plywood top, then apply a few braces to keep the dowel and the plug perfectly vertical.

against the 38 mm by 89 mm to form the appropriate indentations along the aft side of the lead keel. These are important details.

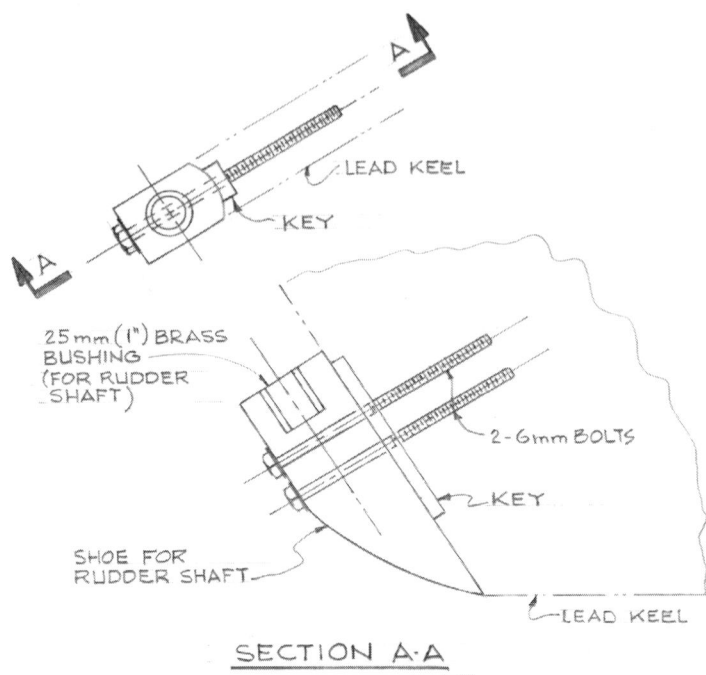

FIG.#17 'SHOE' FOR RUDDER SHAFT

When selecting a suitable spot for digging the ground hole, keep in mind that hot lead will cause severe explosions on contact with water or even the slightest amount of moisture. Select a spot that is well drained and free of ground water. For the same reason, plan to do this work during the dry months. For example, I dug the hole and poured the concrete in April and waited till late August before the lead was poured. Concrete takes a minimum of twenty eight days to cure and considerably longer to lower the moisture content.

The thickness of concrete that is poured around the male plug should be no less than 75 mm. I embedded reinforcing bars in the concrete. However, if the soil or ground is firm and undisturbed that is probably not necessary. The relatively small amount of concrete required can be hand-mixed using crushed rock and washed sand (navy jack) and

Portland cement, available at most building supply centres. Mix the navy jack and cement at a ratio of 3:1 or even 4:1. While pouring the concrete, air pockets or honey combs can be avoided with frequent tamping.

After chipping out the styrofoam the concrete mould must be measured for volume to calculate the keel's total weight. Melt some lead of the type and weight you will use for the keel. Pure lead weighs 708 pounds per cubic foot but you are not likely to find pure lead and therefore your lead will weigh a little less. Measure the weight of the lead to be used by volume. Fill a five-litre container with molten lead and weigh it. Now fill the concrete mould with water[21], five litres at the time, to establish total weight. The required weight is 1,900 pounds.[22]

In the case of *Lady Jayne* volume had to be reduced by nine litres. A small plywood box was built and suspended into the mould. This nine litre cavity is *Lady Jayne's* bilge. It is an excellent place to store water entering the cockpit while under sail. Stored deep down in the keel, bilge water will cause neither rot, nor wet feet. The Dragon is a wet boat because of its low free board and can readily take on significant quantities of water when sailed in a breeze and through chop.

Before the mould is ready for lead, one interesting but very precise job remains – the big bolts that attach the lead keel to the hull must be placed in their exact location. Even with the assistance of pilot drill holes (see Dead Wood, Chapter Four) these six bolts may not be perfectly in line with each other. The angle at which they enter and exit the lead keel will vary slightly from bolt to bolt. The challenge is to suspend the bolts over the lead keel mould in their precise position and angle.

This is how I did it, but there is most assuredly a better method since two of my bolts did not line up and for those two I had to enlarge the pre-drilled holes - a very messy job.

I used two pieces of 12 mm plywood, sufficiently long and wide to cover the lead keel mould, separated and held together by some blocks

---

21    Do this far, far ahead to allow the concrete drying time before pouring, lest the resulting explosions scar the concrete surface and send hot lead flying all round. Also, moisten the concrete, soaking it several days before measuring its total volume. Dry concrete will absorb moisture and yield an inaccurate measurement.

22    See Lead Keel, Chapter Four.

38 mm by 140 on edge. Place this over the hull and drill the holes from inside the hull through both layers of plywood. Remove from hull, place additional 38 mm by 140 mm blocks on edge on the plywood surface that was against the hull, place and fasten a third layer of plywood on these blocks and drill from the opposite side through the two layers of plywood already drilled. Drill into and through the third and last layer that has yet to be drilled. Keep this last layer of plywood fixed to the one in the centre, discard the other. You now have a template for mounting the bolts in their respective holes. This template is placed over the mould aligned with the Centre Line. The bolts will extend into the mould about 300 mm and kept in place with nuts fastened against the template. If this operation is done carefully it should line up the bolts with their pre-drilled holes perfectly, at least in theory.

Also, on each bolt put one nut at the end that goes into the lead. It is extra insurance against the relatively soft lead stripping the thread and compromising a bolt's holding power.

Concrete form with jig holding bolts that
fasten lead keel to hull. Tank to melt lead over open fire

Your mould is now ready to receive the lead. Garden Bay Marine machine shop loaned me an old fuel tank and a 40 gallon drum, the latter cut into two halves. The tank was just large enough to hold the entire quantity of lead needed. It is important to pour the keel all at once. It prevents structural weakness and a pockmarked surface. The fuel tank was welded up with four legs of simple angle iron sufficiently high off the ground to have a good wood fire underneath. A hole was cut in the bottom of the tank and a nipple for 37 mm steel pipe welded on. From there the steel pipe was extended to reach the concrete mould.

It is best to place the tank and fabricate the steel pipe such that the lead can be poured at two locations. I poured into a central location and found the lead cooling off before it reached the two ends. A torch had to be applied to facilitate flow.

I inserted a ball valve in the pipe not far from the tank but in addition with the aid of a few elbows and a short nipple the pipe could be swung into an upward position to form a standpipe. This prevents the hot lead from draining until this section of pipe is lowered into position. It turned out to be wonderful foresight since the ball valve developed a leak long before I was ready to pour. Most ball valves have a thin inner plastic lining which dissolves under the built up heat. With the ball rendered useless, the standpipe saved much trouble. Alternatively use a gate valve; it has no rubber or plastic inside parts that can melt. If you rely on a standpipe, have on hand a blow torch to quickly heat the lead in the standpipe when the entire cauldron of lead in the fuel tank is ready for pouring. Lead inside the standpipe will cool and harden when there is no flow.

The drum halves are placed one on each side to contain the heat. Then a good wood fire is built underneath. Slowly start feeding in quantities of lead wheel weights. As the lead heats and melts, the metal clips and all other impurities float to the top where they are easily skimmed off with a metal sieve. Smoke and foul odours will rise from this witches stew but do not fear lead poisoning. Lead poisoning is not an issue until the boiling point, which is far higher than the melting point. It took nine hours to melt all the lead and about ten minutes to pour. I had collected the wheel weights over several years from many different tire stores and stored them in plastic buckets.[23]

Near the bottom of several buckets some moisture lingered on the lead. This can be dangerous, since on contact with hot lead any moisture causes immediate explosions, splattering hot lead in all directions. Wear protective gear. Better still, ensure all lead is bone dry.

At all times stand clear from danger and anticipate what may happen. For example, I had not anticipated the strength of the stream of molten lead as it spouts out of the standpipe when lowered. It overshot the mould, scattering lead into puddles on the gravel beside the mould before the flow could be directed into the mould. Fortunately, no harm was

23    The waste of rubber and clips is about 15% in weight. So, collect more than you need.

done. But what if someone had been standing right there? In hindsight, an elbow at the end of the pipe to direct the flow down into the mould would have been much safer. Fortunately, the slabs of lead decorated with rocks, sand, and gravel could be dumped back into the tank where all that is not lead floats to the surface for easy removal. Since lead is so heavy, rocks and metal objects float on the surface - a most peculiar sight.

Nine hours to melt, ten minutes to pour

Such a quantity of lead does not cool quickly; the next morning it will still feel warm to the touch. Let it cool completely before attempting to turn out the ready rod bolts. As it cools, the lead will shrink ever so little, making it easier for the rods to be turned out. Even then, 18 mm diameter rods do not twist out easily. A nut welded to the top permits a lot of force. On this nut I used a heavy duty crescent wrench, its arm lengthened to two metres with a steel pipe; even then it took two persons to turn and extract the rods. After the first extraction, turning them in and out gets easier and can be helped with a dab of grease.

Extracting the lead keel from its concrete mould is difficult. I tried, unsuccessfully, to lift it out with a front end loader. The concrete surface is pockmarked from tiny air pockets trapped between the styrofoam mould and the inflowing concrete. These tiny pockets are clearly noticeable when the styrofoam is removed. I am not sure they can be filled without causing the filler to melt in the hot lead. The tiny air pockets fill with lead and prevent the keel's extraction. The concrete must be broken and chipped away from the lead, a bit of a job. That is when I regretted placing reinforcing bar into the concrete.

Lifting the keel up and out can be done by machine or with some digging and a come-along. Moving it into position under the hull requires placing the keel into a cradle. The cradle consists of two, 38 mm by 242 mm planks clamped or bolted together fore and aft of the keel and projecting just below the keel's bottom edge. The cradle will keep the keel upright and provides a straight bottom surface on which to roll the cradle and the keel into position. Get a good supply of 37 mm, or 50 mm steel pipe about 300 mm to 500 mm in length to be used as rollers. If the surfaces are smooth, straight, and clean such rollers will move very heavy weights with minimum effort. Positioning and keeping the rollers ninety degrees to the direction the object is to travel will ensure a straight course. Steering to the left or right requires moving the leading rollers slightly off ninety degrees. In addition, for this job a good come-along and a few hydraulic jacks are indispensable.

Cradle to move lead keel on rollers

## Turning the Hull

Before the lead keel can be fastened to the underside of the hull, another interesting project must be carefully planned and flawlessly executed – turning the hull right side up. Planning must consider safety for workers and structural soundness to prevent undue twisting or strain on the hull. Fortunately, for centuries boat builders have turned hulls and perfected this challenging operation. Many different methods have been devised and can be found in the vast boat building literature. Differences relate to size, weight, and type of construction of boat, plus location. For example, *Lady Jayne's* cold-molded method of hull construction, together with the temporary, inside bracing at each of the frames, makes the hull substantially rigid, even at this early stage of construction. That is a plus. But the hull's location inside a confined space posed a special challenge – how to turn in one spot? After much reading and reflection, this is the method I followed.

At this stage the hull without the lead keel probably weighs 1,000 to 1,200 pounds, which is relatively light. However, it has considerable bulk to be balanced and controlled at each stage of the turn.

Following the procedure below *Lady Jayne* turned on a dime, almost effortlessly, in a fully controlled manner all through the turn, free of scary moments. A friend came to assist, but in retrospect one person can turn this hull single-handedly.

Construct one cradle at Station Five and one at Station Eleven. These cradles are each shaped to form a large half-wheel on either port or starboard. The half-wheel commences its segment of a circle about 150 mm below the 38 mm by 89 mm collar tie at the Construction Line and ends about 975 mm above the Sheer Line at Station Five. To be identical, each half-wheel's segment of circle has to be of the same diameter. The full circle's diameter is about 1,250 mm. Construction of the cradles should be as shown in figure 18.

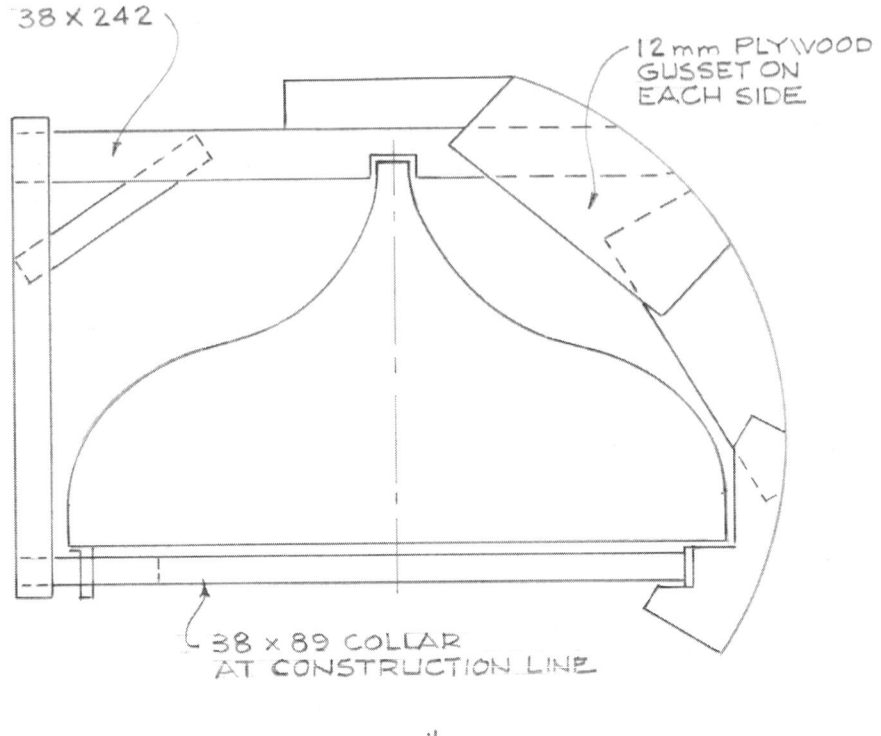

38 × 242

12 mm PLYWOOD
GUSSET ON
EACH SIDE

38 × 89 COLLAR
AT CONSTRUCTION LINE

## FIG. #18
## HALF WHEEL FOR TURNING HULL

The distance from the Centre Line to the outside of each half-wheel should be the same. Once in place, connect the two half-wheels with substantial cross bracing so the two will form one cradle. At Station Eight on the opposite side of the hull from the half-wheels fashion a lifting eye. To lift the hull use a come-along attached to the rafters above. Spread the load over several rafters, just as the lifting eye should be attached to the frames of Stations Seven to Nine. At the rafters attach the come-along to a point directly above the hull's Centre Line.

To roll the hull while maintaining the same location, place a 38 mm by 242 mm under each cradle wheel. Level and secure this plank so that it will not move. Then place several lengths of steel pipe on this plank and on top of those another 38 mm by 242 mm of about 1,800 mm length. This shorter length will ride to one side as it follows the half-wheel's surface. It is then replaced by a second 38 mm by 242 mm of similar length while the steel rollers are continuously moved one at the time from one end of the plank to the other as the hull rolls over.

Before turning can commence, the 38 mm by 89 mm support legs that hold up the hull are cut just below the collar tie at the Construction Line and the hull temporarily supported. Then attach the come-along to take the weight on one side, remove the legs, and lower the other side such that the half-wheels rest on the guiding planks. Start lifting with the come-along and soon the half-wheels will start to take over and move the hull. After reaching the halfway point the come-along is slowly released and the hull will settle into its correct, right side up position. Jack the hull up to create sufficient height and a clear path for the lead keel to be moved into position underneath. In addition, after the lead keel has been attached the rudder and its long shaft need to be inserted into the shaft's standing pipe. This requires considerable additional clearance under the hull, unless, as in the case of *Lady Jayne's* boat house, the dirt floor allows for digging a hole of sufficient depth. After calculating the required amount of clearance, level the hull across its beam, block the hull, and brace for support to keep it upright, remembering the lead keel is yet to be moved into place. Do not impede its path with blocking or braces.

Roll the lead keel into position on the steel rollers and jack up to within about 18 mm of the hull. Ensure lead keel is perfectly plumb. Insert the ready rods from the inside of the hull, after placing a washer under the nuts, through the pre-drilled holes into the lead keel's threaded holes. If all the calculations and templates are correct each of the six bolts should line up perfectly. If not, as was my lot, some of the pre-drilled holes may need to be enlarged and the additional space filled with epoxy after the keel has been firmly attached[24]. When all six bolts are threaded in, squeeze a generous amount of 3M 5200 caulking compound in the 18 mm space

---

24      This is easier said than done. First, enlarge those holes using a larger diameter bit. Second, bring the lead keel up to the hull, caulk and tighten bolts that line up. Third, because you are using ready rod, the remaining bolts need to be replaced by new bolts about 75 mm longer and, like the original, have a nut welded on one end. Fourth, turn these in as far as possible. Fifth, cut bolt to remove welded nut, pour epoxy into space around bolt making sure to leave no air pockets, turn on a new nut on top of a washer and tighten.

between the hull and lead keel, jack the keel up to the hull, tighten bolts and scrape off excess caulking compound. 3M 5200 caulking is the best on the market, not only as a waterproof seal but also for its adhesive quality.

Preparing to roll hull

**Rudder**

The rudder blade is constructed by laminating stock 37 mm by 37 mm of soft wood such as Douglas Fir. The shape and dimensions of the blade are as per Construction Plan. To shape the thin trailing edge use an electric plane, grinder, and sanding for the final finish. The blade is attached to the 25 mm diameter stainless steel rudder shaft with three sets of flanges or straps of thin stainless steel plate about 50 mm wide welded to opposing sides of the shaft so the blade can be fitted in between and bolted through. Use plenty of epoxy filler to shape the round leading edge around the shaft and over top the holding straps. Then finish with fibreglass, one layer of six ounce cloth and two layers of epoxy resin.

At its bottom end the rudder shaft is held in place by the 'shoe' attached to the bottom of the aft edge of the lead keel (fig. 17). This lead 'shoe' needs to be poured and that requires a mould. Make the mould a little wider and larger than needed so once poured the 'shoe' can be shaped to fit the contours of the lead keel at this point. Lead is soft enough to be planed, chiselled and sanded.

To receive the rudder shaft embed a bronze bushing of 25 mm diameter and 31 mm length in the lead 'shoe'. To prevent the lead from entering the bushing from the underside insert a 25 mm dowel into the bushing with enough length protruding from the opening to remove the dowel after the pour. To prevent the bushing from turning, rough up its outside surface before pouring. After the pour, drill for the two, 6 mm bolts that will attach the 'shoe' to the lead keel. These bolts, and especially the key, ensure the very considerable sideway forces of the rudder will not dislodge the 'shoe' and the rudder shaft it holds.

At the top end of the rudder shaft a special attachment is needed for attaching the tiller.[25] That attachment should be obtained at this time since it will require that the rudder shaft be cut at a severe angle and at the appropriate distance above the deck to suit your particular attachment. In addition, it may require a key be machined into the rudder shaft or at least a hole drilled to receive a through bolt.

And finally, the shaft will need to have a hole drilled for the through bolt that will hold in place the round collar of hard, dense plastic needed just underneath the block of similar hard, dense plastic that surrounds the rudder shaft where it penetrates the deck. This collar prevents the rudder shaft from riding up and escaping the bronze bushing at the bottom. All such machining on the rudder shaft is best done before the shaft is attached to the blade.

Before attaching the rudder you may wish to treat the lead keel surface with a filler epoxy and a good sanding to eliminate all the tiny imperfections and make the surface perfectly smooth. Then lay up a 200 mm wide strip of fibreglass all around across the joint of hull and lead keel, followed by another coat of epoxy resin and final sanding.

---

25    I purchased a perfectly good tiller attachment second hand at a mariners exchange shop at considerable savings.

After attaching the lead keel and inserting the rudder, lower the hull and block it up level on its water line and level across its beam. Since the hull need not be moved from now till that happy, far off day when it leaves the boathouse for its launch, select its location within the workshop carefully and block the hull solidly.

Take a moment to relax and enjoy the satisfaction of seeing your exceptional project take shape. Particularly, walk around to admire the Dragon's lovely lines. Congratulations! Your careful planning, many varied skills, hard work and persistence are all on display. You have put yourself, all your energy, into it and it shows. Progress is evident, revealing to all your personal skills and talents. Close your eyes, listen attentively, hear the wind in the sails, the waves against the hull, feel a stiff breeze, the Dragon's tender response and in your mind's eye sail away to a far horizon, a future of adventure enriched by deep satisfaction in a job well done.

## CHAPTER SIX

# COAMING, DECK, ENGINE, CUDDY, SEATS, AND SOLE.

"The perfection of a yacht's beauty is that nothing
should be there for only beauty's sake."
John MacGregor

With the lead keel and rudder attached, the hull turned right side up, securely blocked up and supported, the temporary inside bracing can be removed and the deck beams or joists installed. All the inside bracing can be removed with the exception of the 38 mm by 89 mm collar ties at the Construction Line for Stations Three, Six, Eight, and Twelve. This will the prevent distorting the sheer lines until enough of the deck beams are in place so that these last braces can also be removed.

For each station fore and aft of the cockpit and cuddy roof, laminate a deck beam using three strips of oak - 15 mm by 37 mm. Halfway between each station laminate an additional deck beam using two strips of oak, also 15 mm by 37 mm. The deck beam immediately forward of the cuddy roof and cockpit coaming is located 55 mm forward of Station Six. It will fasten against the aft side of the uprights that brace the mounting beams for the Upper and Lower Stays.[26] The beam immediately aft of the cockpit coaming is located 300 mm aft of Station Eleven. Since these two beams support considerable weight, they should be constructed out of with three strips.

Follow the Construction Plan in determining the amount of crown at Stations Six and Eleven; then, at the Centre Line, string a mason's line from Station Six to the stem and from Station Eleven aft to the transom. Each deck beam crowns at the mason's line. Since the curvature is very

---

26    See Fittings for the Stays section, Chapter Four.

slight the lamination can be done in place by fixing a temporary support at the Centre Line from the keelsom up to the underside of the deck beam and bending the oak strips on top of this support. At each station secure the beam ends against the rib with a small "knee" of 5 mm thick gussets on each side. The in-between-station beams are secured against the Sheer Batten with a 15 mm by 37 mm support on the underside, and of course epoxy. As always, check for fairness and place additional temporary supports as necessary.

The upright supports aft of the cockpit remain permanently in place. They should be slightly off center to accommodate the sheet and double blocks required to tension the backstay. Also, the upright support under the first beam aft of the cockpit needs to be considerably stronger than the others. On it will be mounted the double blocks and cam cleat for the backstay sheet as well as a pivot for the idler arm that controls the free running wheel to pressure the v-belt that drives the propeller shaft (fig. 19).

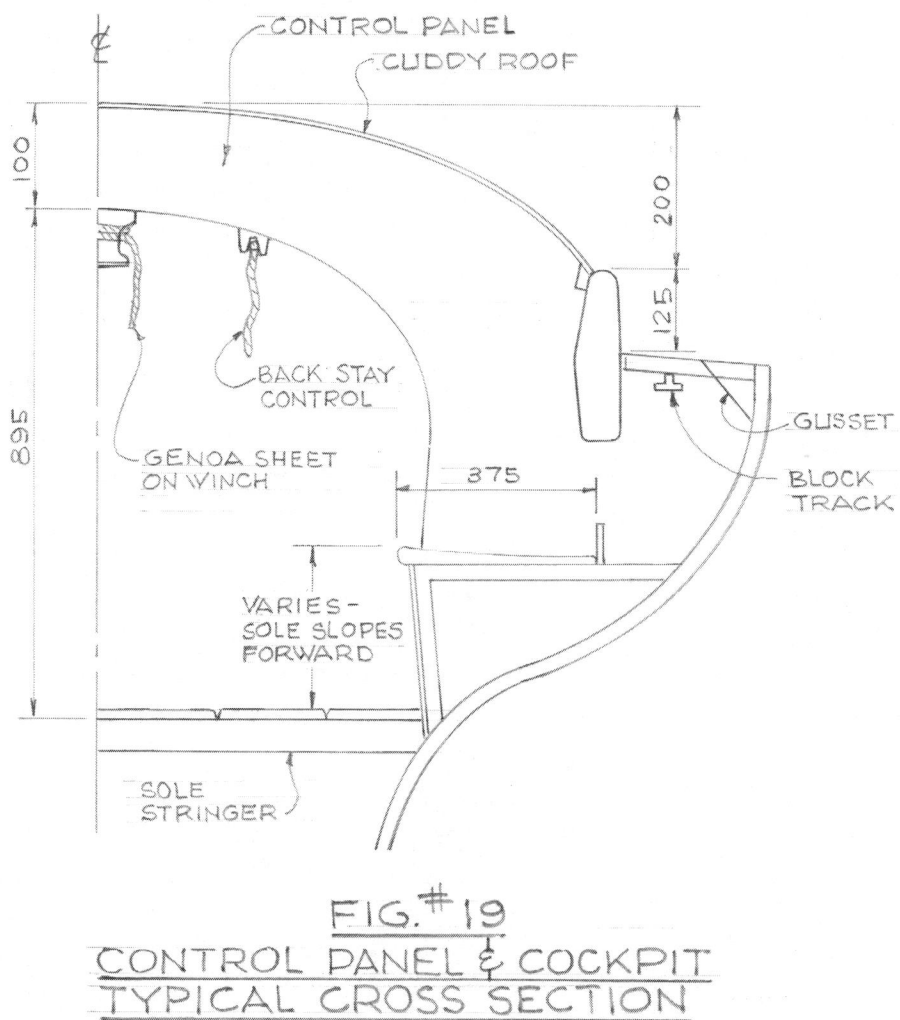

CONTROL PANEL
CUDDY ROOF
100
200
125
895
BACK STAY CONTROL
GENOA SHEET ON WINCH
375
GUSSET
BLOCK TRACK
VARIES – SOLE SLOPES FORWARD
SOLE STRINGER

FIG.#19
CONTROL PANEL & COCKPIT
TYPICAL CROSS SECTION

## Coaming and Deck Beams

**W**ith the deck beams in place you have determined the length of the cockpit and cuddy areas at their longest point which is at the Centre Line. This distance is somewhat arbitrary. In the case of *Lady Jayne* the cockpit is enlarged aft to accommodate the engine and ensure it will not be under the deck. An air cooled engine in particular requires maximum ventilation. If so desired, these areas can be made greater or smaller.[27] If the boat is to be sailed for singlehanded racing a more compact cockpit might be best. But for day-sailing and cruising, an enlarged cockpit with comfortable seats should be preferred. In addition much thought needs to be given to the layout of the rigging. Where will the genoa and the running backstay leads run and be tied off? This is the time to make that final determination.

As you have noted, on *Lady Jayne* the cockpit coaming extends to include the cuddy area and is constructed as one continuous ring. The cuddy roof attaches to the inside and top of the coaming. The entire coaming is laminated on the lofting platform, which for this purpose doubles as a construction or building platform. Once completed, it is then fixed in its permanent location and the remaining deck beams along both sides are installed to hold it and the hull's sides in place. The coaming is an integral component giving strength to hull and deck; it needs to be strong.

On the lofting platform loft the sheer lines for the area between Station Five and Station Twelve. Next, loft the outside of the coaming. On *Lady Jayne* the minimum deck width between the coaming and the sheer is 250 mm. This is approximately at Station Eleven. From this point forward the deck on each side of the coaming widens while the outline of the coaming still follows the gentle curvature of the sheer lines. At Station Eight the deck width is 285 mm and from there widens appreciably towards the front of the cuddy roof. The corners on the aft side of the *Lady Jayne's* cockpit are generously rounded for aesthetic appeal, nor do these rounded corners interfere with the seats since the seats stop 300 mm short of the aft end of the coaming. The aft 300 mm of cockpit is reserved for the engine cover. That cover needs to be raised above the seat level. You have now lofted the exact outside dimensions of the coaming at deck level.

The thirty coaming jigs (see fig. 8 in Chapter Two) are screwed onto the lofting platform 50 mm inside the coaming lofting line and at ninety

---

27    However, if the boat is to be registered and given a number, the International Dragon Association's rules must be followed without deviation.

degrees to the lofting line. As an exception, at the Centre Line along the forward edge of the coaming place a jig 74 mm inside the line and taper the shape of the coaming on both sides of the Centre Line such that at 600 mm from the Centre Line the jigs are again set back 50 mm. The coaming is built up by laminating, one layer at the time, sixteen layers of 3 mm mahogany plywood. The plywood is cut 300 mm wide. For bending the plywood in the corners some of it should be cut across the grain making those sheets 300 mm by 1220 mm. For laminating use Titebond II, apply with a roller, and clamp generously. Between jigs, clamp the plywood layers between battens on either side. Do three layers at any one time and let it dry overnight before continuing. As usual, stagger the joints. Finally, add an additional eight layers of 3 mm plywood strips, 1220 mm long, at the forward end of the coaming.

Jigs to form coaming, set in place on lofting platform

After completing the lamination lift the coaming into place, fasten temporarily and all around mark the deck level. Note: the deck level is 12 mm above the beams. Because of the deck's crown in the beam dimension and the sweep of the deck for and aft no segment of that line will be straight; the line follows the contour of the deck. Move the coaming back into the workshop. Now mark the top edge. From the deck line measure up 100 mm all around. The 100 mm will be exposed above the deck. That establishes the top of the coaming. The coaming's top edge thus follows the gentle flow of the deck contour all around. Cut off all excess stock.

From the top edge of the coaming make the coaming 225 mm deep for the cockpit section, and under the cuddy roof forward of the control panel the coaming is 137 mm deep. Now cut off all along the bottom. The coaming around the cockpit needs to be reduced in thickness below the deck beams to reduce weight. Mark on the outside a line 137 mm from the top. Stock below that line needs to be removed to a depth of 18 mm, thus cutting a rabbet along the bottom outside, reducing the thickness along the bottom of the cockpit section to 32 mm. What remains is to shape the profile or cross section of the coaming.

For shaping the cross section of the coaming there are no fixed rules other than function and aesthetics. The function is that it serves as comfortable backrest for the cockpit seats and aesthetically it must avoid a square and box-like appearance. *Lady Jayne's* coaming is shaped as follows: along the top edge the centre-most 15 mm wide stock is left. Mark this with two lines. These lines are centered on the top edge, except at the forward end of the coaming, where the coaming is much wider, draw those lines parallel to the inside of the coaming. This will leave more stock on the outside where the coaming is widest. From those two lines taper to full width at 100 mm down from the top for the cockpit segment. Do this for both the inside and the outside, except do not taper the inside for the cuddy roof segment. In this segment remove stock only on the outside.

For the cockpit segment, the inside lowest 100 mm is tapered at the same angle as the top 100 mm. The two tapered surfaces do not meet in a point. The 25 mm flat area along the center of the inside is now slightly rounded. The result is easy on the back and adds grace to *Lady Jayne's* appearance. For removing this much stock use a grinder or heavy duty disk sander and finish with much sanding by hand. The top 15 mm wide edge should be rounded both on the inside and the outside for the cockpit segment and only on the outside for the cuddy roof segment. The bottom, 15 mm edge is rounded on the inside only, for the cockpit segment.

Stand back to admire the graceful lines and rounded profile of the coaming. Notice that the angle of the taper on the outside, above deck at the forward end is more acute than the other sections. This more pronounced taper lends a streamlined profile to the front of the cuddy roof and is the reason why the coaming is built up much wider at the front. It is such relatively minor details that give the *Lady Jayne* its sleek, pencil thin appearance.

The taper exposes the end grain of the plywood. To attain a hard, mirror smooth surface coat the entire coaming surface generously with epoxy sealer three or four times with vigorous sanding in between coats. Repeat until all cavities are fully sealed with epoxy. Since the coaming is very visible and finished with a high gloss paint, all surfaces should be faired to a mirror-like smoothness. Apply a thick layer of filler suitable for out doors use and compatible with the paint product that will be used for the finish and sand heavily. Keep doing this until all low spots have been filled and high spots sanded out. Finish with 220 grit paper.

The coaming can be painted and completely finished before it is installed in the hull. Finishing it now avoids all the cutting in, making painting so much easier. To attain a very high gloss it is best to wet-sand the paint between coats with 400 grit emerald cloth sandpaper.

Here is a practical tip for wet-sanding. Mix a little dish soap into the water. Without soap the wet sanding cloth clings to the painted surface making the movement of the sanding block more skip and jump than smooth slide and glide.

The *Lady Jayne's* colour scheme offsets the dominant deep, red wine colour of the hull's mahogany surfaces with the green trim of the coaming. Red and green are complementary and pleasing. However, not any green will do. It needs to be a very deep, dark green bordering on black. To attain the most perfect shade of deep green mix the highest grade of Benjamin Moore marine paint in their darkest green with the same high grade product in black.

Mix paint with paint; do not, as is often done, mix paint with a colour compound. Mixing paint with paint delays fading, it will hold colour much better than a base paint mixed with pigment.

When mixing for that perfect shade of deep green, keep adding black until the rich, vibrant shine is dulled towards grey. At that point back off, add some green, there is too much black. You have gone too far; the colour has lost its vibrancy, it has turned lifeless and dull. Keep dabs of paint from the various stages of the mixing process side by side on a sheet of white paper. You will note the progression and at which point it degenerates into grey. It is best to observe the colours outside in strong daylight. The same green should be on the waterline and the ornamental Dragon on the bow stem post. These are the only painted visible surfaces. Do not use a primer, instead dilute the paint for the first two coats and apply five to seven coats in total.

The coaming is a prominent and highly visible component. When finished to perfection its rounded corners, tapered sides, and graceful lines contribute significantly to the overall appearance. In addition, it provides comfortable seating and structural strength. Time spent to construct the coaming well, is time well spent.

With the coaming in place the remainder of deck beams can be installed. Next, provide extra support around the pulpit and rudder shaft. Both locations need reinforcing of the deck framing to withstand the huge sideways pressures, particularly at the mast. The rudder shaft has a hard plastic collar where it penetrates the deck This can be a 50 mm diameter plastic dowel with a 25 mm drilled hole for the shaft. It should be about 100 mm long and drilled very precisely for a snug fit. That collar should be surrounded by a solid block of wood, itself an integral part of the deck framing, and firmly secured with some stainless steel screws to prevent any turning and lifting.

This hard plastic collar in effect is a bearing in which the rudder shaft turns. This collar/bearing is cut about 25 mm above the deck at an angle parallel to the deck. Under the deck it is cut just below the deck framing at a 90 degree angle to the shaft. The collar/bearing rests on the preventer collar, which is also of hard 50 mm diameter plastic and about 50 mm long. It in turn rests on the rudder shaft's standpipe. As mentioned in Chapter Five, this preventer collar needs to be bolted to the shaft and acts to prevent the rudder shaft from rising and lifting out of the "shoe" at the keel that anchors the bottom end of the rudder shaft.

## Rigging and Blocks

The *Lady Jayne's* rigging is purposely hidden below deck to give a clean uncluttered look above deck. She has no winches, blocks, cleats, and running gear in sight. All running gear is below decks, except the genoa leads which are partially above deck. They show above deck from the genoa clew to where they disappear into the deck over a fixed block located under the deck just off the fore end of the cockpit. Since these blocks are fixed, their exact location both fore and aft and their distance from the sheer are critical.

For the *Lady Jayne* these distances are as follows: the aft side of the fairlead block is 2825 mm aft from Station Four, measured at ninety degrees to the Station Four line. It is 192 mm from the Sheer Line to the centre of the block.

To minimize possible breakdown I used plastic sheaves instead of wood on these two blocks. Install these blocks now with plenty reinforcing. They are very difficult to reach after the decking is installed. For detailed information on block construction see Blocks section, Chapter Seven.

Fixing the fairlead blocks to attain an uncluttered deck limits the ability to adjust and trim the genoa for varying wind strengths. This loss of sail trim adjustment can be partially compensated by sewing a cord and small cam cleat into both the genoa leech and foot to adjust the tension on leech and foot under varying wind strengths.

The running backstays enter the deck near the transom over steel blocks fixed below deck and then attach to a set of double wooden blocks with the control sheet exiting a cam cleat at the dashboard under the cuddy roof. The forward double block is fixed against the inside of the sheer batten at Station Eight, one for each side, and the second double block travels aft along a hardwood track fastened to the underside of the deck beams between the hull and the coaming. The aft block needs to travel approximately 1350 mm to accommodate releasing the running backstay when the boat is running before the wind with the boom and mainsail swung out. These blocks and tracks need to be installed prior to the decking.

To provide daylight under the deck, a prism might be installed in the deck forward of the mast. If so, appropriate spaced blocking needs to be installed between the deck beams.

The backstay also travels below deck. A steel block needs to be fixed just below deck where the backstay enters. Attach a second steel block to the attachment bolted into the keelsom earlier (see Chapter Four). Attach a single block to the aft side of the coaming and a cam cleat to the centre support just aft of the coaming (fig. 20).

## Cuddy Roof

The shape and construction of the cuddy roof is limited only by your imagination. *Lady Jayne's* is kept reasonably low, streamlined, and rounded. The height is largely determined by the convenience of managing the control sheets that emerge from under the control panel. This includes the genoa fair leads and the two running back stays. The genoa fair leads run over a small winch mounted at the Centre Line, upside down, behind and just below the control panel. The same winch is used for both sheets. The winch is mounted on an angle so as to receive the leads from blocks, one on starboard, one on port, mounted forward and lower down. To the left of the winch is a wooden cleat mounted on the face of the control panel to tie off the sheet when under sail.

The running backstay sheets run over a block forward of the control panel and through a cam cleat mounted upside down just behind and under the control panel, one for starboard, one for port. The under side of the control panel, where the sheets emerge, should be high enough so that standing on the cockpit sole managing the sheets does not require undue bending down. While racing in close quarters managing the various sheets at the control panel is a constant job. Ease of operation and efficiency are of primary importance. In *Lady Jayne* the distance from the cockpit sole to the underside of the control panel at the Center Line is 895 mm. From there it is a further 100 mm to the top of the control panel at the Centre Line (fig.19).

In addition, it is possible, and perhaps prudent, to have the halyards for both sails end and cleated at the control panel. The *Lady Jayne's* halyards end and cleat below decks on the pulpit support. They run through rope clutches positioned on the pulpit and are tensioned with a winch also mounted against the pulpit supports. The advantages of bringing the halyards to the control panel are clear. It is easier to raise sail. But more importantly, it offers increased safety in the event it is necessary to shorten sail and bring either sail down because of a sudden, unexpected squall. This is particularly significant when sailing singlehandedly. In the case of *Lady Jayne*, to bring down a sail the skipper needs to not only leave the rudder to go forward but, in addition, must duck under the cuddy and crawl to the mast's pulpit. It takes longer and therefore increases the risks during wild and unpredictable conditions.

Don't think it will never happen because it will. Even inside Pender Harbour where the wind can swing wildly striking from various directions *Lady Jayne's* rudder has been overpowered and rendered useless by gusts of just 30 knots. Under such chaotic conditions it is best to take down sail quickly.

When the front sail is hanked to the fore stay, as is *Lady Jayne's*, it is prudent to run a thin cord from the sail top through the hanks to the cockpit to bring down the sail to deck level after the halyard has been released. The front sail is not likely to come down much at all in a strong blow and no one should venture on deck near the bow in heavy winds.

The Dragon has no railings, not even a rub strip at the sheer, and a wet varnished surface is slippery as green sea weed on boulders along the shore. It is prudent to have control lines accessible from within the cockpit.

Having determined the height and shape of the cuddy roof the control panel can now be constructed. When faced from the cockpit this panel is concave. From the two ends at the coaming it curves inward 185 mm deep at the Centre Line. At the coaming it curves and reaches down to be flush with the underside of the seat covers. It ends under the deck in a vertical line even with the backside of the coaming, that point will also be the back side of the seat covers. From that point it measures 300 mm laterally, and from there it arches up to measure 100 mm at the Centre Line. Make a pattern from stiff cardboard. Using the pattern as a guide, construct a building jig to shape the curvature needed to make the dash concave. Laminate 5 layers of 3 mm plywood and then cut the shape according to pattern. Later, line the side facing the cockpit with book-matched mahogany planks, 3 mm by 75 mm. Cover the grain ends with mahogany veneer.

The cuddy roof itself consists of four laminated layers just like the hull. The inside and outside mahogany layers run fore and aft. For the inside layer use 6 mm thick planks tapered towards the front with a tiny v-joint separating the planks. For the outside layer use 3 mm thick planks, book-matched, and again tapered to the front. The thinner stock is rec-ommended for the outside to prevent sun heat from warping the surface planks. The in-between layers are 3 mm plywood strips run diagonally. The lamination can be done in place. During construction it will require a temporary support structure in addition to the control panel. The mahogany planks must be fitted and shaped carefully, particularly where they butt into the coaming. Where necessary provide permanent support battens on the inside where planks and coaming meet.

Before laminating the final outside layer, construct and install on the underside the winch mounting block. This winch must withstand a substantial sideways force and should be braced, bolted, and anchored thoroughly before the final layer is applied. It is best to spread the load over a large area.

Finally cut the roof line at the cockpit end. This line is also concave when viewed from the cockpit. The curvature is 37 mm deep at the centre. The roof line starts with a 50 mm overhang at the coaming. Cover the grain ends with a mahogany veneer.

## Engine and Through-Hull Fittings

Before proceeding with the decking it is prudent at this stage to coat the entire inside, including the deck beams except for their top edge. *Lady Jayne* is finished inside with *Varathane* clear oil. There are those who suggest that totally encasing wood in epoxy could eventually weaken the wood fibre. With that in mind, I chose the oil finish. Oil is also easy for treating scuff marks and light scratches.

There are three through-hull fittings – stuffing box, engine exhaust, and bilge water. All three require ample epoxy as caulking. The 17 mm diameter bilge hose runs through a hand pump[28] located between the engine and the port side, aft towards the transom where it exits above the water line. The engine exhaust is located at the water line straight aft of the engine. Since this engine is not water but air-cooled, the pipe is very hot and requires a custom designed through-hull fitting to match the 25 mm diameter stainless steel exhaust pipe. The fitting is double-walled for about 100 mm up from the hull. Here the inner wall is full of small holes through which the exhaust escapes, but the end is welded shut. A boat in motion generates a quarter wave which ensures the exhaust fitting is washed by water and kept from overheating. The many small holes in the side wall, instead of an open end on the exhaust pipe, help prevent water splashing up and possibly entering the engine.

---

28      I had bought a hand pump long before it was installed and when several years later I finally tried to work it, it failed to suck up any water. After much trial and error I greased the suction rubbers and it worked immediately.

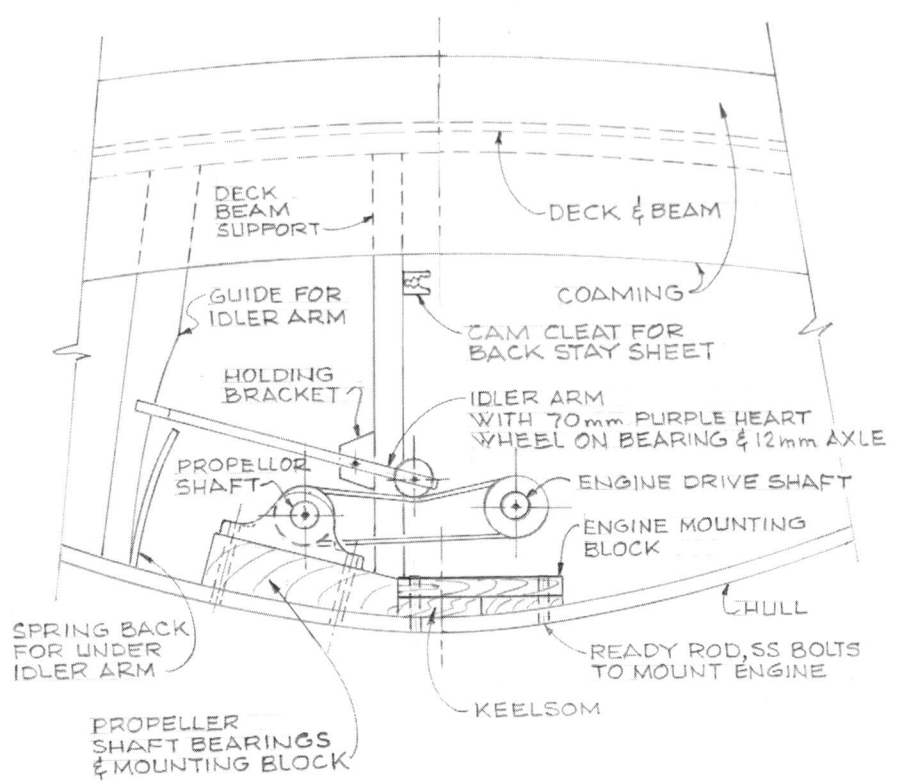

DECK BEAM SUPPORT

DECK & BEAM

GUIDE FOR IDLER ARM

COAMING

CAM CLEAT FOR BACK STAY SHEET

HOLDING BRACKET

IDLER ARM WITH 70mm PURPLE HEART WHEEL ON BEARING & 12mm AXLE

PROPELLOR SHAFT

ENGINE DRIVE SHAFT

ENGINE MOUNTING BLOCK

HULL

SPRING BACK FOR UNDER IDLER ARM

READY ROD, SS BOLTS TO MOUNT ENGINE

KEELSOM

PROPELLER SHAFT BEARINGS & MOUNTING BLOCK

FIG.#20 CROSS SECTION - AFT OF COCKPIT

The exhaust pipe is also custom made. It rises straight up from the double-walled, through-hull fitting to within 50 mm of the underside of the deck beams, travels forward towards the engine where it plunges down to within 50 mm of the hull, from there it bends up to the engine manifold. At the lowest point is a small drain with a gate valve[29] and near the manifold is a larger gate valve on the exhaust pipe itself. This larger gate valve is to prevent salt water entering the engine. In rough conditions water could splash up and enter the exhaust pipe, particularly when the engine is not in operation. As a preventive measure, whenever the engine is not running the large valve is shut. The small valve is opened

---

29    Gate valves do not have any rubber or plastic parts that could melt from the heat of the exhaust.

only when water needs to be drained out of the pipe. The entire length of pipe is wrapped in asbestos-like cloth and in addition a protective heat shield is installed between the pipe and the deck beams.

*Lady Jayne's* engine has run for five hours continuously without overheating, but again, an air-cooled engine is not generally deemed acceptable. I do not recommend an air-cooled engine for any boat, let alone a wooden one. I only report what I have done, knowing the risks.

Next, fashion and install the idler arm and its supports (fig. 20). The propeller shaft bearings can be mounted. The stuffing box can now be temporarily attached to its mounting block. The propeller shaft exits through the stuffing box and is then supported by a stainless steel strut which must be bolted against the hull. Ensure the bolts are richly embedded in epoxy and supported by a plate on the inside of the hull. The propeller runs through an oil-less bearing welded to the strut. To prevent electrolysis place a zinc on the propeller just fore of the strut. The distance between the zinc and the strut should equal twice the zinc's diameter. If placed too close, the zinc will prevent water from entering the oil-less bearing. Check that everything is aligned correctly before permanently mounting the stuffing box.

## Decking

Before applying the decking ensure all the beams and stringers are faired to perfection. Any dips or high spots will always be noticeable and cause of irritation. A gleaming deck with the light showing a mirror smooth, even surface will always delight. The first layer of decking is 6 mm marine grade, five-ply plywood.[30] Fit the sheets in place, mark all the beams and stringers from the underside. Then remove the sheets and drill from the underside between the lines for plenty of 30 mm long screws. Next paint the underside white with a high grade marine paint or epoxy before permanently installing the sheets with epoxy and screws. The screws are

---

30    *Lady Jayne* used Aqua-tek, Occume 6mm, 5-ply 20 lbs. per sheet

countersunk and then filled with epoxy filler lest they work loose and cause mischief.

The final layer of decking on the *Lady Jayne* is 5 mm thick stock. Mahogany planks, 75 mm wide for along the sheer, adjacent to the coaming, and middle or King planks and 42 mm wide Yellow Cedar for the remainder. Since these planks follow the curvature of the sheer lines they need to be steamed and bent. To bend the sheer planks is very challenging. Because the planks are thin, they'll want to buckle under pressure. Preventing this requires a special jig. The jig needs to be 4.88 meters long and provide a snug slot between two layers of 25 mm plywood to prevent buckling. To bend two planks at the time, make the slot 11.5 mm deep and a little under 75 mm wide.

The 11.5 mm dimension may seem more than needed but while steaming, the stock swells slightly. Since I had not anticipated this, it had to be redone.

When wood bends under pressure the fibre on the inside of the bend compresses and on the outside the fibres are stretched. To preserve the edges, pressure should be applied along the entire surface, both along the inside and along the outside. Thus the jig has to have a concave and a convex member for its entire length. These are brought together with clamps. No clamps should touch the subject planks. To preserve the correct curvature one of the members can be screwed down on the building platform together with the plywood cheeks that prevent the buckling. It is best to over-bend since there will be considerable spring-back.

Place some 38 mm by 89 mm lengths between the jig and building platform to facilitate clamping. Such spacers also allow for clamping the two plywood cheeks together should they part under pressure. It is difficult to bend planks that thin in the width dimension but with a reasonably straight grain, a very precise jig, and many clamps it can be done. For steaming use PVC pipe with plenty of holes to let the steam travel along the stock. One or two hot water kettles will generate sufficient steam.

The first two sheer planks I did were loosely held down in place on the deck after the bending and left to sit for a few days to dry. That was a costly mistake, for they cupped; probably because the increased moisture content picked up during steaming evaporated faster on the exposed surface.

Laminate the planks permanently in place immediately upon removal from the bending jig. Once they have cupped it is impossible to undo. I had to start over. These sheer deck planks are placed over the top hull plank which needs to be planed flush with the deck plywood. To press down the sheer planks use many jigs temporarily screwed into the deck beams and stringers. Use wedges between the jigs and the plank. Next install one mahogany plank all around the coaming. All joints are spaced 3 mm to be filled with black epoxy later. The fish-tailed King planks are left for last.

The in-between areas are covered with the Yellow Cedar planks spaced 3 mm apart. It is possible to leave the plank surfaces rough and to then sand the entire deck surface after the joints are filled with black epoxy. However, I dressed the plank surfaces before installation, then filled the joints and did all the sanding needed to remove excess epoxy. I used Industrial Formulators Titanium Surface Finish epoxy mixed with black colour compound. It has the lowest viscosity and a working life of 48 hours after mixing in the hardener. The low viscosity allows the epoxy to run like water filling in any remaining cavities between the planks and plywood subsurface.

It makes for a very solid deck. In a hot burning summer sun the deck attracts a lot of heat and unless the planks are absolutely perfectly laminated to the subsurface planks might lift. The drawback of a product with low viscosity and long working life is soon evident when filling the joints. Since no part of the deck surface is perfectly level the epoxy will run to the lowest spots and there overflow. The answer is to fill the joints in small sections at any one time. It is a tedious and time consuming process, requiring much sanding to remove excess epoxy. The reward is a solid deck and very appealing to the eye. The black epoxy joints between Yellow Cedar provide a sharp and striking contrast.

Where the Yellow Cedar planks meet the King plank the ends are rounded to give the King plank its fish-tail shape. The King planks are left for last and consist of two book-matched mahogany planks, each 75 mm wide. To cut the precise shape make a pattern of heavy paper, this is taped over the surface, marked with crayon, then cut out.

Marking pattern for King Plank. Dragon ornament on stem post

## Seats

The seats start at Station Eleven and run forward to end against the control panel. The seats should be hinged to lift up for storage underneath. The seats consist of seven Western Maple planks, 50 mm wide and 4 mm thick laminated on 6 mm marine plywood with a small v-joint separating the planks. Give the seats a slight curvature across their width. The curvature is cut into the three or four battens underneath to maintain the curved shape. Lengthwise, the planks follow the contour and shape of the coaming. With dried Western Maple it is quite difficult to steam and bend this lengthwise curvature, therefore consider cutting the planks out of wider stock. Along the front laminate a bull nose and along the back a batten, 9 mm by 72 mm. For hinges, along the bottom of this back batten affix two blocks holding a chunk of dowel 37 mm diameter and about 50 mm long. Let the dowel turn in a hole drilled through 6 mm hardwood attached to the underneath frames. It works perfectly, doesn't rust, and costs little beyond your time.

The front under the seats consists of 3 mm Maple plywood set in a frame of 12 mm by 55 mm rails. The fronts slope in to provide more foot room at the sole level and again, it all follows the curvature of the coaming. The bottom rail is level with the top of the sole, while the top rail is 210 mm below the bottom of the coaming. Very light, simple frames both support the tops of the seats and fix the fronts in place. The space under the seats is used for storage of bumpers, sheets, clothes, refreshments, etc.

For holding the seat lids up when needed, fix a light support leg that folds against the underside halfway down their length. Let one end turn on a wooden dowel and support the other end with a magnet mounted into the underside of the seats and a screw mounted into the support leg.

To cover the front of the engine, provide a sliding panel of 3 mm Maple plywood between the seat fronts at Station Eleven. When running the engine that panel needs to be removed and laid aside or stored underneath. The cover for above the engine can be made similar to the seat tops with a solid board of Maple along the front to raise this area about 100 mm above the seats. It too, must be easily removable and placed aside to operate the engine.

## Sole

The sole boards rest on stringers, one at each set of ribs. The elevation of the stringers is as follows. The top of the first stringer at the aft side of the mast pulpit is 65 mm above the keelsom. The top of the last stringer at Station Eleven touches the hull where the seat fronts end. Between those two points the sole has a gentle slope down to Station Seven, there the stringer's top is 800 mm above the keelsom. The stringer at Station Ten will need to withstand a much greater force since the traveller is attached to it (or so it is in *Lady Jayne*).

Normally the traveller is at deck level, or just below it. Placing the traveller between the seats flush with the sole boards makes the cockpit more user-friendly but shortens the traveller's length making it more difficult to keep the boom centered when close-hauled. Again, it is a choice between comfort and performance. It is a judgment call. I chose comfort, but there are good reasons to forego comfort in favour of performance. I have not found performance affected significantly. However, if the boat is primarily for racing, comfort should be sacrificed for performance. *Lady Jayne's* traveller has stops held in place by a spring loaded plunger. These must be moved manually every time the traveller's position is changed. It is more cumbersome than a sheet-controlled traveller.

Remember, a prime consideration was to give *Lady Jayne* an uncluttered, simple appearance. This entails choices involving sacrifices. A sheet-controlled traveller is more effective and easier to operate but also requires additional tackle and clutter.

*Lady Jayne's* sole consists of two sets of boards, one relatively small for the area aft of the traveller and the other covers the entire space from the traveller to the mast pulpit. The sets of boards are made up of bookmatched mahogany planks, 150 mm by 5 mm, laminated to Sitka Spruce stock of the same dimensions. I used Sitka Spruce because I had it available but also because it is very light in weight and with a tough fibre.

Early aeroplanes used this wood species for that reason. The individual planks are spaced 3 mm apart and held in place by a few battens underneath and some brass screws into the stringers at a few key points. Make these boards easily removable for maintenance and the annual cleaning of the bilge section.

The seats and sole have a bright finish with the mahogany stained like the hull. On these surfaces I did not use epoxy but *Varathane* Classic Clear Oil-based Spar Finish. At the beginning of each season after cleaning and a light sanding another refresher coat is applied.

The dragon ornament is cast out of lead but hollow to cut weight

# Chapter Seven

# Mast, Boom, Blocks and Bright Work

"Life is too short to splice wire rope."
Bernard Moitessier, circumnavigator and author

"Any idiot can do it."
Nick Benton, master rigger

These extreme, diametrically opposed sentiments about splicing wire rope can also apply more generally to building wooden boats. For many, building a wooden boat from beginning to end seems too complex and time consuming, to even begin. But with practice comes familiarity and those with more experience may view their craft as quite ordinary. The truth lies somewhere in between. The amateur wood boat builders to whom this book is addressed do well to remember that confidence grows along with progress made and experience gained. At completion you may not exclaim, "Any idiot can do it!" but it does get easier. Building the mast and blocks take patience and persistence, but it is entirely possible for most, while the result – unique products each with a high level of function and beauty - is deep satisfaction.

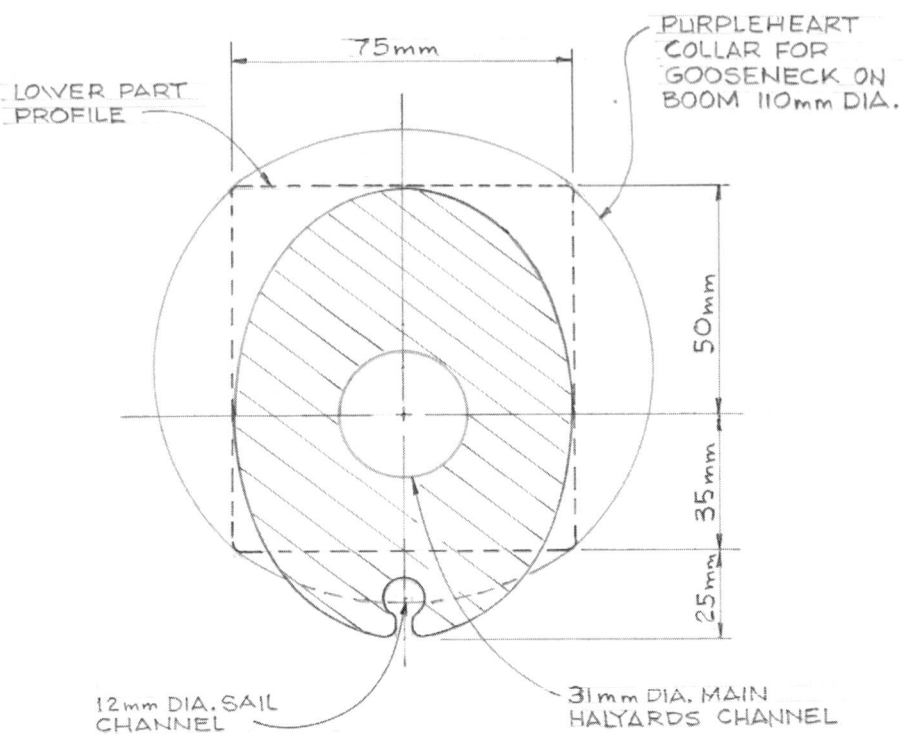

75mm

PURPLEHEART
COLLAR FOR
GOOSENECK ON
BOOM 110mm DIA.

LOWER PART
PROFILE

50mm

35mm

25mm

12mm DIA. SAIL
CHANNEL

31mm DIA. MAIN
HALYARDS CHANNEL

# FIG.#21 MAST CROSS SECTION

The mast is made out of Sitka Spruce. This species is lightweight, bends easily, but is also very tough. It is also pleasant to work with, particularly if you are fortunate enough to obtain straight, close-grained stock. In the early decades of the 20th century Sitka Spruce was widely used for aeroplane construction because of its unique properties, but today there is little use for dimension Sitka Spruce lumber, hence it is not easily available except from specialty wood suppliers. I was fortunate to obtain two pieces 50 mm by 240 mm, 8 meters long, perfectly straight, free of any imperfection and best of all with a very close grain of 16 growth rings per 25 mm. It came from a tree that must have been at least 200 years old.

That tree was growing to be *Lady Jayne's* mast when the explorer Simon Fraser paddled down the river that bears his name in 1808. Knowing the source of your raw materials adds uniqueness to your project. Your boat will be one of a kind.

The mast consists of two halves laminated down the centre. Keep these halves rectangular and rough until after lamination. Dressing the mast into an oval shape is done later. While 8 meter is a long length of stock the mast is longer and therefore requires a scarfed joint for each half, one near the bottom the other near the top. The scarf joint should be at a slope of no less than 12 to 1. The mast has two round channels, one for the halyards, and one for the sail slides (fig. 21). When determining the diameter of the large centre channel make the walls of the mast not less than twenty percent of the diameter. Depending on what you wish to use for halyards, 31 mm diameter for this centre channel is probably about right. The depth and width of the slot leading to the sail slides channel or groove are critical; consult your sail maker, in particular, check the shape and width of the sail's headboard. It might have to pass through this slot all the way up. Of course, both these channels are routered before laminating the two halves. The mast has a tapered section toward the top, as per plan. For the top one-third of this tapered section the halyard channel is also reduced. Since in this mast section there is just one halyard reduce the channel from 31 mm diameter to 9 mm diameter. Near the lower end of the mast the sail channel stops 300 mm above the Black Band to provide access for hoisting the main sail. From this point down the mast's fore and aft dimension is reduced and the oval cross section gradually transforms into a rectangular cross section. That transition is complete at 100 mm above the Black Band and stays that dimension from there down.

The Dragon mast is a finely engineered product. The mast's greatest pressure point is at the upper spreaders. At this point the following meet and are attached: the jumper struts, the two running-back stays, the higher shrouds, the forestay, and the front sail halyard. To attach these, a special stainless steel collar needs to be fabricated. Centered at the front it wraps around 70 percent of the circumference of the mast and should be about 190 mm in length. The collar is mainly kept in place by three, 7.5 mm bolts, one of which doubles as the axle of a 37 mm diameter steel sheave for the front sail halyard.

There is enormous load and downward pressure on this collar. To lessen the possibility of the bolts tearing into the wood grain, place a steel sleeve around each bolt for the width of the mast. Make these sleeves just a fraction longer than the width of the mast to prevent the collar's edges from digging into the wood surface when under pressure.

Placing sleeves around the bolts is a very important detail which I omitted originally. After just one season the collar had dug into the wood and needed to be redone. After enlarging the holes and inserting the sleeves the problem is solved. The jumper wires and the top of the lower shrouds are attached to the mast with stainless steel straps of 8 mm wide flat bar, slightly bent out. These are fastened to the mast with 6 mm diameter machine bolts, again surrounded by a steel sleeve that protrudes slightly above the surface to prevent the straps from digging into the wood. Install the collar and all mast fastenings after the mast surface has been fully finished. In addition to the bolts, use a generous layer of 3M, 5200 caulking between the collar and the surface. Fully finishing the surface before installation and adding the caulking are important in preventing moisture from penetrating the wood underneath. Water leak troubles that lift the epoxy and varnish finish always start at the fastenings.

While the collar installation must wait, the exact location of the front sail halyard sheave must be determined at this stage, the holes for its axle bolt drilled, and space for the steel sheave chiselled out of each half. Before laminating the two halves, coat the two channels with three coats of epoxy sealer.

Constructing and laminating the mast is done on the special brackets along the inside of the boat house wall as discussed in the Boat House and Workshop section of Chapter Two. Laminating requires many clamps. Additional clamps can be cut from truck tire inner tube. Such inner tube bands can apply a surprisingly heavy load when twisted and then held in place. During clamping, care should be taken that the stock remains perfectly straight in both dimensions. Generously lather both halves with epoxy because clamping such heavy stock can easily leave small air pockets between the two surfaces. Also, take great care to align the front sail halyard sheave precisely without clogging it with epoxy.

To wipe any excess epoxy out of the channels place a thin rope down the length of each channel before laminating. Immediately after clamping use these ropes to pull a wad of cloth back and forth through the channels. In the main channel this thin rope will also be needed later to pull the halyards through.

To shape the mast's oval profile much stock needs to be removed. An electric plane is very appropriate for this job. To ensure both sides are perfectly symmetrical, cut a pattern of one half of the cross-section. Use this pattern as a guide. Mark the centre line for both sides on the pattern. For sanding, take a sanding belt, 600 mm to 800 mm in length, attach a handle to each end, wrap the belt half around the mast and pull back and forth across the grain. That works beautifully, just watch your knuckles. To facilitate the turning of the boom's wooden goose neck against the mast when under full sail in a strong wind, a 150 mm long section of the mast needs to be round with a diameter of 110 mm. Laminate slabs of Purple Heart against each of the four sides of the mast, centered on the lower Black Band, and shape till it is round. Below this, two small boom supports are laminated, one each for starboard and port. Later, after varnishing is finished, cover the tops of these supports with a thin layer of leather.

The mast top requires a special fitting (fig. 22). While the drawings do not call for a halyard guide, *Lady Jayne* does have such a guide on the aft outside as indicated on figure 22. The guide virtually prevents the possibility of jamming the halyard at the top of the mast – the bane of sailors. Also, use some brass ready-rod to affix the assembly to the top of the mast as follows: drill pilot holes, chuck a length of ready-rod in an electric drill, turn the ready-rod into the wood, then cut the ends flush with the surface. Brass is sufficiently soft to be chiselled and sanded. Turning ready-rod into hardwood yields surprisingly strong holding.

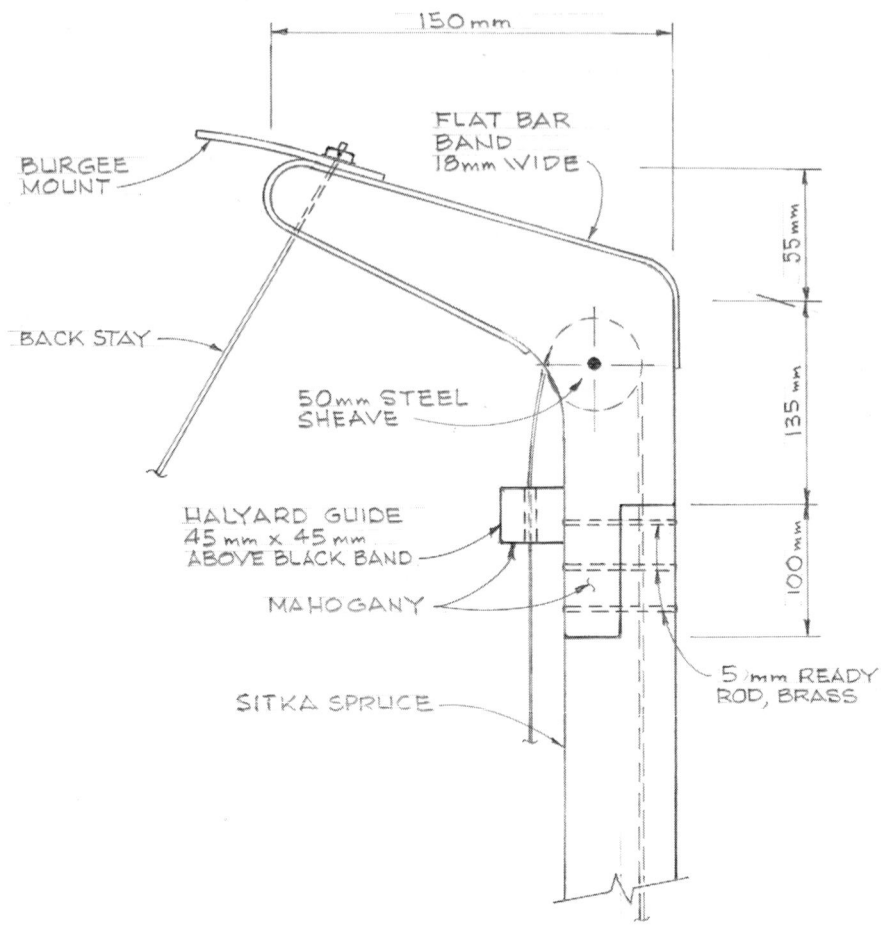

FIG.#22 TOP OF MAST ASSEMBLY

Next, construct the lower spreaders. It is entirely possible to construct these and the jumper struts out of wood. On *Lady Jayne* both are made of Purple Heart. Select stock that is absolutely free of any tiny splits, if in doubt insert a spline. The ends of the struts that attach to the mast are reinforced with two short lengths of brass flat bar. At the mast they attach with a 9 mm bolt into a steel u-channel, 37 mm in length. The opposite ends against the shrouds are widened and fastened with stainless steel wire. The lower spreaders should swing freely to follow the shrouds as the mast bends under various conditions and points of sail. In contrast, the jumper struts do not swing, they need to be fixed to restrain excessive mast bend at the top under heavy winds.

Jumper struts also out of Purple Heart

Raising and lowering the mast requires a pivot point near the top of the pulpit. For that purpose, install two, 25 mm diameter Oak dowels, one for each side drilled into the mast ending just shy of the centre channel and protruding sufficiently to be flush with the outside of the mast pulpit cheeks. Then cut the bottom of the mast very precisely. The cut should slope slightly towards the aft side to let the mast turn on the dowels and yet, seat firmly at its base once it is up. Experiment with a pattern to get the arc just right. Finally, a brass eye-strap is installed on the fore side, 90 mm above the lower Black Band. It will receive one end of the whisker pole when in use.

The two halyards run through rope clutches mounted below deck on the mast pulpit. At this point the halyards are 9 mm rope. With the sails hoisted, the halyards above the rope clutches are 7 x 19 flexible steel wire to minimize stretch. The two sections of a halyard - rope and steel wire - are spliced with a Tail Splice. Tail splices may seem like a deep mystery but can be mastered with some persistence. Detailed descriptions of how to construct this splice are readily available in special rigging and some knot making books.[31] Alternatively, a simple approach requiring no splicing is to use low stretch, polyester braid, or V-100 Vectran Double Braid for the halyards. But do expect some stretch which may prevent attaining perfect sail trim particularly on the front sail.

## Boom

The boom is constructed similar to the mast but without a centre channel. Before laminating the two halves make the following preparations. At the aft end prepare to install a sheave in the centre about 70 mm in diameter for the outhaul sheet. Mount this sheave on an axle that enters each half from the inside only. That looks much better than running a bolt through the outsides but best of all it prevents moisture from penetrating the finish.

To stop moisture from getting under the finish, also seal the surface between the sheave and the boom stock before laminating. Attention to such details will pay huge dividends in years to come. If, as in the case with *Lady Jayne*, this sheave is a wooden sheave, treat it thoroughly with epoxy sealer or raw linseed oil before installation.

Just aft of the outhaul sheave embed in the centre lamination a chunk of brass flat bar to protrude 50 mm above the boom. Drill a 9 mm hole in it from which to attach the boom to the back stay while raising and lowering the main sail.

At the mast end of the boom cut a rabbet 6 mm deep by 45 mm by 200 mm on each side to receive the goose neck. The boom can be laminated, shaped and dressed. Then shape the two halves of the Purple Heart

---

31      One of the best texts is: Brian Toss, *The Complete Rigger's Apprentice: tools and techniques for modern and traditional rigging*, International Marine, 1998

goose neck and fasten with epoxy and three, 6 mm bolts, countersunk and plugged. Two lengths of brass flat bar are installed at the centre of the goose neck near the aft side of the mast. They protrude about 50 mm both above and below the goose neck and are placed 18 mm apart. On the upper side drill a 6 mm hole for a brass bolt which will hold the main sail clew. In addition, on one side the bolt will also hold a small sheave for the Cunningham sheet. The brass flat bar on the under-side should be drilled for a Clevis pin or Fast-pin to attach the boom down-haul which runs down to the pulpit where it is tied off.

On one side of the boom mount a cleat, cut from Purple Heart stock, to tie off the Cunningham sheet. At the underside of the boom mount a similar cleat to tie off the Outhaul sheet. Attach these cleats with two countersunk and plugged screws plus epoxy. At each side of the boom, 1100 mm back from the mast, mount one half of a cleat to attach the boom restrainers.

Boom restrainers prevent the boom from unexpectedly swinging through the cockpit when running downwind. A swinging boom can cause considerable discomfort (or much worse) to any heads that fail to duck in time.

Boom restrainers consists of two, 7.5 mm diameter ropes, one for each side, that run from the boom through the deck opening of the upper shrouds to a cam cleat below the cuddy roof. At the boom end of the restrainer fashion a loop, called an eye splice[32], sufficiently large in diameter to be hitched around the two half cleats, one on each side. These half cleats should be angled against the side of the boom in line with the angle of the restrainer ropes.

After the final finishing coat, apply a small patch of leather on each side where the boom rubs against the upper shrouds when full out. For details about shaping the brass attachments for the boom vang and traveler sheets see the Blocks section below. The flat bar brass attachment for the main sheet is located on the boom directly above the traveler and the boom vang attachment is located on the boom 830 mm aft of the mast. The main sheet attachment needs to swivel both sideways and fore and aft and be designed accordingly (see picture front cover).

---

32      For detailed instructions on how to make an eye splice, consult any book on rigging (see footnote 31).

Instead of a Spinnaker, *Lady Jayne* is equipped with a Whisker Pole to hold the genoa's clew out and suspended. A whisker pole is not as flexible as a spinnaker but very useful when running downwind 'wing-on-wing'. Again, it is a trade-off between simplicity and performance. My experience suggests a whisker pole is not a substantial disadvantage over a spinnaker, particularly in winds 12 knots or greater. The whisker pole, about 32 mm by 25 mm and 2900 mm long, can be laminated with three or four layers of Mahogany and Sitka Spruce stock. Laminating such a thin pole adds strength but also appeal. Select stock to provide a sharp contrast. One end is pointed, or spiked for insertion in the foresail's clew and the other end attaches to an eye-strap at the front of the mast. A 25 mm diameter latching end-fitting, commonly used on spinnaker poles, is attached to the pole with about 100 mm length of 25 mm diameter copper or stainless steel tubing secured with epoxy. The pole is stored when not in use either on the deck, or against the mast. If stored on deck, mount a small eye formed out of Purple Heart on the deck just aft of the stem post. This eye will take the pointy end while the latching end of the pole is snatched around the lower shroud at deck level. After finishing the surface, glue small patches of leather in three places on the under-side of the pole to protect the deck against rubbing.

It works perfectly. The pole is always within reach and the latching end is easily disengaged. It should be possible to place or remove the pole in seconds while under sail, particularly when single-handed. While rounding the windward mark during a race, the speed of setting the front sail with the whisker pole determines your place at the finish line. But never leave the cockpit to go on deck without a safety line.

## Blocks

Building authentic wooden blocks that function well, that stand up to load and weather, and retain their beauty is particularly satisfying, perhaps because it is so seldom done. *Lady Jayne's* wooden blocks include the following:

- Two sets of double blocks with a cam cleat inside, one set for the main sheet and one for the boom vang.
- Two sets of special double blocks for the running-backstays. One set on each side, one double block of each set is attached to the sheer batten and the other runs aft along a fixed track below deck. (See Rigging Blocks section of Chapter Six)
- Seven single blocks for running-back stays, front sail fairleads, backstay, and the Cunningham.
- Four sheaves: for the boom outhaul, the Cunningham sheet and two at the bottom of the pulpit for the halyards. For the latter two, see Mast Pulpit section of Chapter Four.

The cam cleat blocks (fig. 23) are a special design to accommodate the teeth section cut from a normal, hard plastic cam cleat. When aligned properly these improvised cam cleats are quick to set and release; they work beautifully. These are a great help, particularly at the main sail sheet and boom vang.

The design of these cam cleat blocks provides the convenience and performance of modern technology while concealing the curse of modern life - the tedious, bland sameness of plastic, chrome, and stainless steel.

As figure 23 illustrates, the brass straps take all the pressure and load. Brass is soft and bends easily with relatively little heat. Make a jig for bending brass flat bar. The jig should be able to hold, vertically, a number of different diameter steel rods, 200 mm in length, parallel to each other, but at different distances from each other. Some are set apart no further than the thickness of the brass flat bar. It is useful if these bars can be inserted and extracted, as needed. A common blow torch used for plumbing is sufficient to heat the brass. Brass can be brittle and break under bending if too hot, or not warm enough. It takes some practice. After bending the flat bar for the blocks and having gained some experience, try bending the straps attaching the main sail blocks to the boom and finally the most challenging of all – the straps on the boom for the boom-vang block. The latter are on an angle and to shape the correct angle requires holding the flat bar at an angle between the jig rods while bending. It is often difficult to predict the exact length of the straps before the bend is in place. Fortunately, most straps will have ends that need to be cut to length. Therefore, cutting to length as well as drilling the necessary holes is best done after shaping the flat bar straps.

While brass straps look good and are strong, rope strops or grommets can be used instead. In that case, a rope grommet must be formed and laid out of three-strand rope.[33] Within that grommet, at either one end or both, an eye is formed by a brass or bronze thimble held in place with sail maker's waxed whipping twine. As well, the grommet is embedded in a shallow grove around the body of the block. In this type of construction the load transfers from the sheave axle to the block's cheeks. It is acceptable but without the benefit of metal, not as strong and can't be expected to last as long.

Next, cut and shape the sheaves. Sheaves can be plastic, ready made and bought, or handmade. If handmade, there is a further choice between wood or various composite products that resemble impregnated canvass and may be available from a bearings shop.

I probably should not recommend wood sheaves but for the purists wood may be irresistible. Wood is amazingly durable. The Netherlands has three hundred year old windmills whose moving insides resemble the gears, wheels, and cogs of a Swiss watch. All those parts, teeth, axles, and gears made entirely of wood have been in motion labouring under a load for over three hundred years.

*Lady Jayne's* sheaves are out of Purple Heart and have stood up well. After six seasons there is no need to replace any of them. However, there is a possibility that the wooden sheaves develop splits and then crumble. It is paramount to select perfect, close-grained stock and to thoroughly treat the wood before installation.

---

33    Rope Grommets are explained in most knot books and in Brian Toss' book mentioned in footnote 31.

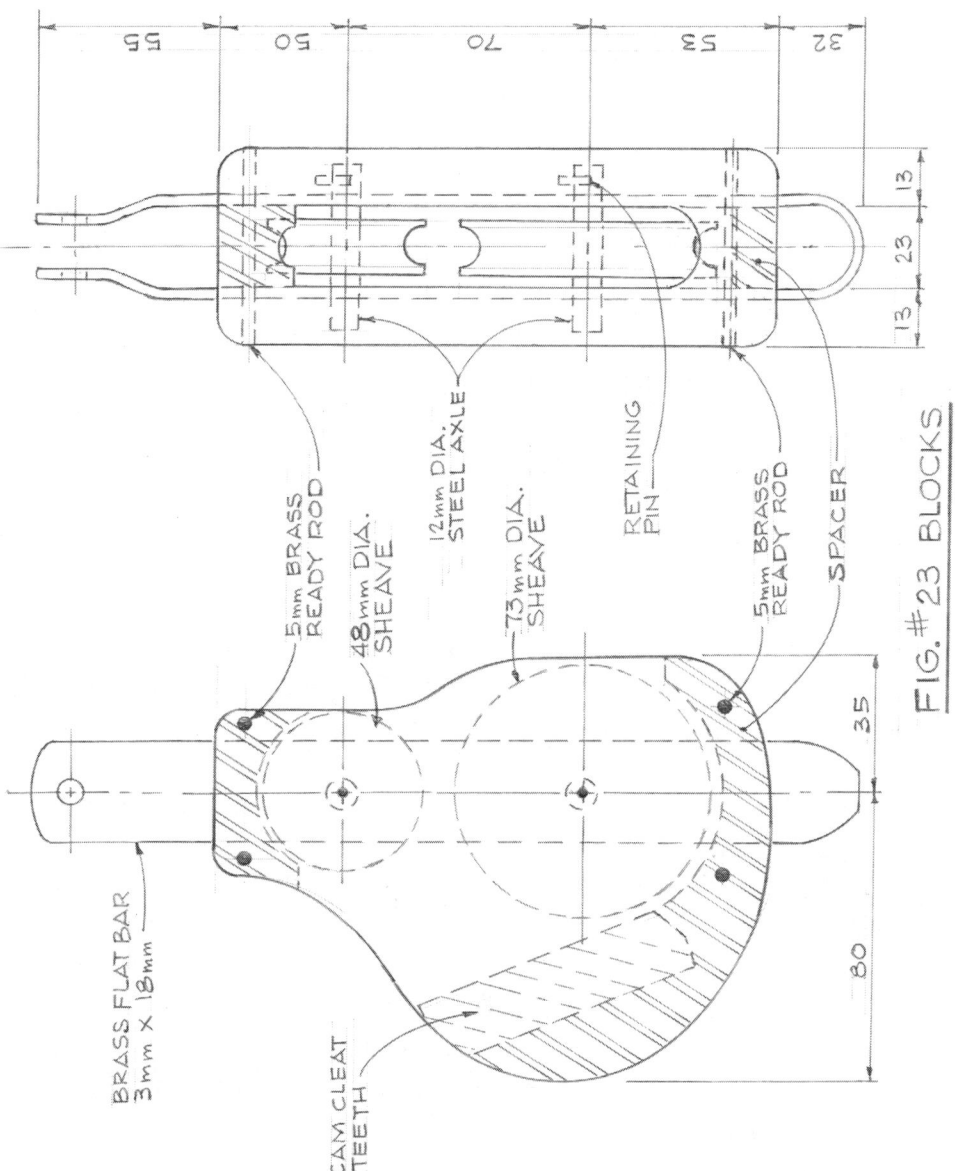

FIG. #23 BLOCKS

The sheaves are cut out of stock with a hole saw chucked into a drill press. The sheaves need a bronze bushing which turns on a stainless steel axle, 12 mm in diameter. The bronze suitable for a bushing is of a special kind, impregnated with oil and acquired from a bearings shop. After cutting the round sheave slabs drill the bushing holes. To ensure such holes are centered with precision cut an appropriate sized circle in a small jig which is clamped on the drill press table to hold the sheave slabs in place for drilling. The bushing tube's outside surface is roughed with coarse sandpaper and glued with epoxy into the sheave slabs. Care should be taken to ensure the bushings are inserted at a perfect ninety degree angle to the sheave surface, lest the sheave wobbles on its axle. To accomplish this, glue up all the slabs at once on a length of bushing tube. First, epoxy the inside hole of the slabs and the outside bushing tube, fix the tube in a vertical position, then stack the slabs on top of each other around the tube with a wooden spacer separating the slabs. The spacers need to be the thickness of a hacksaw kerf. As you place each succeeding slab ensure excess epoxy is removed. After curing, cut the wooden spacer and tube between each slab with a hacksaw, ream out the burr on the inside of the bushings, and clean up the sheave surfaces with robust sanding.

Round and smooth the sheave's rim and carve out the groove for the rope with a gouge chisel on a wood lathe. The sheaves are mounted on a wood lathe as follows. With the bushings glued in place slip any number of sheaves, side by side, over a length of 12 mm steel ready-rod. Place a piece of sturdy scrap paper between each slab to see each slab and guide the gouge chisel when cutting the grooves. This row of sheave slabs is firmly held together between two nuts and washers. For support at the tail head of the wood lathe, drill a shallow hole into the end of the length of ready rod. For the head stock mandrel end, attach to the ready-rod a piece of 50 mm by 50 mm hardwood about 80 mm long. Attach the two by first drilling a hole into one end of the hardwood, dead centre, just under 12 mm diameter, then turn the ready rod into that hole with the help of a dab of oil. Now, start the wood lathe and turn the sheave slabs to shape the groove on each sheave's rim. Finish by sanding the rim and groove while sheaves are on the wood lathe.

Next, cut African Mahogany stock for the cheeks. The width should be a little wider than the finished product. Cut the mortise for the brass flat bar straps on one side of the cheeks. The depth of mortise should be 1 mm deeper than the thickness of the strap. Do not cut the cheeks to length yet. Two long boards from which the cheeks will be cut are placed on top of each other. The spacers, 2 mm greater in thickness than the thickness of the sheaves, are cut and shaped with a groove along the concave edge and then placed in position between the two cheek boards. Precisely mark the centre of each sheave axle and the location of each ready rod, brass pin. Drill a pilot hole for the brass pins completely through both boards. Drill a pilot hole for each sheave's axle through the top board and into the second board but not all the way through, just enough to mark its location is sufficient. And do not move the drill press fence, that precise setting will be required again. After all these holes have been drilled the cheek boards are cut across to each block's length.

Ensuring that all holes drilled and the mortises are perfectly aligned can be challenging. It is helpful for instance, when cutting the mortise on a table saw or shaper, to mark the edge of the cheek board that is against the fence and place those two edges on top of each other before any holes are drilled. When drilling, place the same edge against the drill press fence and always keep the same board surface on top.

To align the holes in the cheeks and those in the brass straps, temporarily assemble each block with the brass straps in place but without the sheave. First, on the top board drill or chisel a counter sink for a coin, brass cap, or leather diamond-shaped cap to cover the axle on one side of the block. Then, using the pilot hole, drill the axle hole through the top board, through the brass straps and into the bottom board, stopping 4 mm from the bottom surface. Keep the straps apart with a temporary spacer. Again to ensure perfect alignment, use the fence setting of the pilot hole drilling.

On most machines it is difficult to reset a fence in a former position, precisely. Keeping it in place until the work is done is the best way to prevent misalignments.

Cut the stainless steel axles to length. To prevent the axles from spinning, drill and insert a short length of stainless steel welding rod as a restraining pin. It should be near one end of the axle and protrude 6 mm from the axle. This end should be at the cap and space for the restraining pin needs to be chiseled just under each cap. Take the temporary assembly apart and remove burr from brass strap holes. Some initial shaping of the blocks, particularly at the top and bottom around the brass straps, should now be done. The blocks are almost ready for permanent assembly. What remains is to coat the insides of the cheeks and the grooves of the spacers with three coats of penetrating, sealer epoxy. Seal inside the mortise, the axle holes, and restraining pin space. The outside finish will remain untarnished provided no moisture can penetrate from inside.

The sheaves should be treated thoroughly with linseed oil. They can be dipped completely and hung to dry. However, rub in and remove all oil that is still wet after thirty minutes, lest the surface develops a skin and subsequent applications do not adhere effectively. Apply many coats; the first two should be thinned significantly. For raw or boiled linseed oil to truly penetrate the sheaves, coat and then steam the sheaves for 30 minutes, remove, rub off any wet oil and let it dry. Oiling the sheaves provides lubrication should a rub develop on the inside of the cheeks. In addition, it is easy to occasionally apply more oil for maintenance. Do not oil the cheek insides and spacers; it will weaken the epoxy adhesive strength. When assembling the blocks for final gluing with epoxy, remove linseed oil from inside of sheave bushing; next, lubricate it and the axle with axle grease. Glue and clamp the cheeks and spacers, then drive in the brass pins.

The brass pins are essential. The cheeks are subject to considerable pressure and held together only by the relatively small surface on the spacers. Pressures and ultraviolet rays conspire to separate the cheeks. The remarkable holding power of ready-rod turned into hard wood will prevent such separation, even if the adhesives let go as most do, eventually.

Now the blocks can be rounded, initially with the band saw, then with a router to knock off the sharp edges and last with a hand plane and much sanding. Glue in the caps. To finish as bright work, first work linseed into the inside of the cheeks and spacers then apply three coats of epoxy followed by seven to nine coats of high gloss spar varnish all around. Such a heavy coating gives good protection against ultraviolet rays and also protects against scratches from ropes scuffing and wear and tear from normal handling.

## Bright Work[34]

In addition to the blocks, the hull, deck, cuddy roof, mast, and boom are all finished with multiple coatings of epoxy and marine varnish. First apply three coats of sealer epoxy, followed by three coats of Clear Coat epoxy resin, followed by six coats or more of marine varnish. Allow epoxy to cure for a week before applying varnish and wash with recommended solvent. Since those solvents are expensive, lacquer thinner, which is just as good, may be preferable. There are many high-end marine varnishes but *Lady Jayne*'s bright work is protected from UV rays by Interlux's Goldspar, a clear, high gloss polyurethane varnish. Some say polyurethane is difficult to apply properly, but that has not been my experience.

Always ensure that your varnish is suitable to apply on top of epoxy. Before applying the first coat of varnish fill any remaining scratches, depressions, and unevenness with a glazing or surfacing compound suitable for exterior use. Then, sand the wood surfaces to perfection, finishing up with 220 or finer grit. Scratch marks lodged in the wood surface will show through epoxy and clear varnish regardless how many coats are applied. Further sanding is required between each succeeding coat.[35] The preparation is more time consuming than the actual application. The reward of thorough surface preparation is not apparent until the last coat has been applied but then it continually bears fruit for years – smiling back at you like a mirror.

Boat houses and workshops are notoriously dusty and require thorough cleansing before starting varnish work. Literally, hose down everything starting from the rafters. By removing all dust from all surfaces you will minimize contaminating the air with dust particles as you move

---

34    Complete texts on all aspects of varnishing include, Brightwork: the Art of Finishing Wood, Rebecca J. Wittman, International Marine Publishing Company, Camden Maine, 1990

35    From my experience 3M products clog the least. #120 grit (216U) Production RN, Paper A wt. Open Coat, Free-Cut for sanding between the first number of epoxy coats after that use between coats #220 grit 3M (415U) TRI-M-ITE FRE-CUT, Paper A wt, Open Coat.

about applying the varnish. You may wish to separate the workbench area from the boat and its area with plastic sheets. Ensure that your clothes and hair are also free of dirt and dust. Allow for several days to dry out the dampness. Depending on the weather and climate it may require some heat. However, some puddles on the ground around the boat during varnishing are an advantage – water seems to attract dust and it surely prevents dust from being kicked up.

Tools and materials for varnishing include the following:

- Masking tape that lasts without turning brittle and difficult to remove. 3M's Green Masking Tape is good.
- Ziploc bags to store masking tape. Storing opened rolls of masking tape in ziploc bags protects the all-important edges of the tape from indentations and prevents soiling the edges with dust and dirt.
- Interlux fiberglass solvent wash #202. Use this to wash the epoxy surface before varnishing and after each between-coats sanding.
- Interlux brushing liquid #333. It improves the flow of the varnish. Depending on humidity and air temperature, the varnish will flow more or less smoothly. It is very important to get the flow just right. Varnish must flow, it should not pull or drag.
- Cone-style paper strainers and pint-sized paper containers. To keep contaminants out and prevent premature aging, do not paint directly from the can.
- A proper paint can opener, rubber mallet, and stir sticks.
- Your favourite brush. Some persons prefer foam brushes. I have tried, but probably failed to master the appropriate stroke. I find a 67 mm wide, natural bristle brush best.[36]
- Sandpaper and sanding blocks with a soft rubber or cork sole. Between coats use 3M's #220, the same as for epoxy. Always store sandpaper sheets such that they cannot curl. Stacked flat between pieces of melamine particle board is best.
- Latex gloves and clean rags.
- Plenty of lighting supplemented with portable lights as needed.

---

36    As for foam brushes, Wittman claims none are as good as the US-made Jen Poly-foam brushes.

As with any painting always keep a full brush but not too full when laying on the varnish. Each application should lay on a thin but even coat. As a rule, multiple thin coats are much better than fewer thick coats. Prevent sags and frequently check back to remove any runs and sags that may develop. Runs and sags do not dry properly and are therefore impossible to sand out. They are best removed with a razor blade.

To avoid imperfections, work a small area at one time. For the first three coats lay varnish across the grain about three brush widths wide, and then tip-off with a nearly empty brush. For subsequent coats, first wet the area with three or four short strokes parallel to the direction of the wood grain, then brush across the grain and finish by tipping with the grain. Always keep a wet edge and work the varnish into the wet area. To keep a wet edge on a large surface use a roller for laying on the varnish and a brush for tip-off. A very large area requires two persons, one for rolling another to do the tip-off. Roll vertically or against the grain, tip-off with the grain. Vertical surfaces require two more coats than horizontal surfaces to obtain the same amount of varnish.

Varnishing like any craft is an art. Using the brush effectively takes attention to detail, appropriate technique, and much practice. When applied properly and with care the varnish will protect against salt water, weather and sun for many, many years provided that each season the bright work that is exposed to the sun is given a light sanding and a refresher coat. Do not ever allow the weather to penetrate below the varnish into the wood. Each year pay particular attention to where fittings are attached. Those are the first places for moisture to enter and do its damage. Use clear epoxy to refresh caulking coatings around fittings before applying a refresher coat of varnish.

When thus maintained the varnish will bring out the wood grain to perfection and keep the wood in its original pristine state and your boat will sparkle like new, year after year. Now that you have a 'floating coffee table' you may be afraid to use it. Don't be hesitant! The thick build-up of multiple layers of epoxy and varnish ensure that minor scratches easily sand out when applying the annual re-fresher coat.

Varnishing, like Judgment Day, exposes all to light, showing every imperfection in your carpentry work for all to see.

Your attention to detail, persistence in watchfully selecting the natural grain for best advantage, deftly achieving perfect joints and fitting lines is on full display, pleasing the eye for years to come.

Annual maintenance ensures the finish sparkles
like new, defying waves, wind and sun

## CHAPTER EIGHT

# WEIGHING ANCHOR AND SAILING TIPS

"... surely man's most beautiful machine."
Derek Lundy, author, speaking of a wind driven ship in *The Way of a Ship*

After many years of meticulous planning and dedicated work your project is almost complete and quickly becoming an outstanding example of what Lundy so fittingly describes as *"man's most beautiful machine."* What remains are some essentials such as rigging, sails, a trailer to transport your craft to water and accessories for safety and convenience.

The tiller and the tiller extension permit for innovation and further expression of individuality. There is no standard design. The tiller has ornamental value. Its prominent location can truly enhance the overall appearance of the boat. Careful selection of design, shape and material is most rewarding. Limitations are effectiveness, durability, convenience and beyond that your own imagination.

It is common to laminate diverse and contrasting woods such as Oak, Mahogany, Maple, Yellow Cedar, and Sitka Spruce. The tiller must be strong. The pressure on the tiller can, under certain circumstances, be remarkably great. *Lady Jayne's* tiller has protective leather on a segment of its underside where on occasion it rubs the coaming. In addition, for convenience when single-handed, consider installing a simple device for locking the rudder. It permits the skipper to go forward for changing or trimming the front sail. A small dowel protruding from the underside of the tiller will hold the tiller when inserted in one of a series of holes drilled into a slat of hardwood about 250 mm long. This is held to the deck by two legs, all of which pivot to be flat on the deck when not in use (see picture). It is simple and most effective. It is my 'autopilot' and I would find it difficult to sail *Lady Jayne* alone without it.

Suspended from coaming a holder for radio and
GPS. Behind coaming the "auto pilot"

The boom needs a support leg to hold up the aft end when the boat is docked and the leg support allows the tarp to be placed over top of and to rest on the boom. Also, the mast needs a support when taken down and placed on the deck. Other accessories include a holder to house both the hand-held VHF radio and the GPS. Construct this holder so it hangs on the inside of the coaming suspended from the top of the coaming (see picture). That allows it to be moved into a convenient location anywhere along the coaming to accommodate the various points of sail. Unless you are sailing off-shore, the GPS is mostly used to determine speed, which is helpful for determining the effect of changes in sail trim.

There are many additional accessories to meet safety concerns and regulatory requirements. For example, an anchor is essential. It may prevent getting stranded on the rocks in the absence of wind and power. For anchor, I recommend a Delta or QCR type.

Throughout I have encouraged you to 'do it yourself', from machining planks to pouring the keel, but there are limits. For most people it is best to turn to professional help for items such as rigging, sails, boat cover, and an adequate and safe trailer.

## Rigging and Rope

For stays and shrouds it is eminently advisable to involve a reputable rigger. Needless to say, it is the rigging that keeps the mast, sail and entire boat upright in wind and waves. Like a chain, the rigging is no stronger than its weakest connection. One faulty splice can topple everything, imperilling the safety of all aboard and causing untold damage. Because *Lady Jayne* is moved by trailer and her mast needs to be taken down, the back stay and two running back stays have a quick-release shackle about 300 mm above the deck. The fore-stay and shrouds penetrate through the deck to their respective fasteners below. The shrouds and strut wires each need a turnbuckle for applying tension.

Rope for all the sheets, outhaul, Cunningham, and restrainers should be carefully selected, not just for thickness and durability, but especially appearance. Since most rope on the market is meant for fibreglass hulls it may require some research to locate rope that complements rather than detracts from the deep, rich natural wood appearance of your unique craft. I settled on three-strand buff polyester.[37]

Three-strand buff polyester is coloured like and has the appearance of a natural fibre rope without its disadvantages. It will not rot, absorb water, lose its strength, or shrink. It has good grip and handling qualities but best of all with its soft natural look it complements historical and classic wooden boats.

It was originally intended for use aboard Tall Ships training vessels. It looks like hemp but it splices easily and can be washed in fresh water.

---

37     Available in Canada from Transat Marine Ltd. Barrie, Ontario

For washing, soak in detergent such as Oxy Cleaner, wrap it in a circle and tie it down, then wash in washing machine with some fabric softener.

## Sails

Sails are the engine that drives your boat and are best made by a profes-sional sail maker. It is helpful to know the correct terminology, not just for discussing your requirements with the sail maker but especially for effective sailing. The effect of the many possible ways to trim the sails must be understood. Understanding starts with knowing the 'geography' of the sail. Sails have three sides or edges– the *foot* is along the bottom, the *luff* is the leading edge and the *leech* is the trailing edge. Sails also have three corners or points – *head* at the top, *tack* where foot and luff meet, and *clew* where foot and leech meet. Finally sails have a belly officially known as the chamber. The chamber can be increased (made fuller) or decreased (flattened) by any number of methods such as the mainsheet, the outhaul, the Cunningham, mast bend, and tensioning the front-stay and halyard. But chamber is also built into the sail.

The sail can be made with a flat luff for speed or fuller for power. It depends on where you sail. Less chamber near the luff gives speed for smooth water but a fuller chamber near the luff yields more power for seas with a heavy chop.

For sail dimensions the official Dragon specifications should be adhered to. Beyond that the most significant questions are whether your Dragon will be used for racing or cruising and under what weather and sea conditions. The sail maker will select materials and all the other options accordingly. *Lady Jayne's* sails are made of dacron 6.5 oz. for main sail and 5.5 oz. for genoa. The genoa is not furled but hanked on, which is less expensive and yields slightly improved pointing. Since there is no adjustment for the genoa leads at the deck, the genoa foot as well as the leech has a sewn-in cord for adjustments. The main sail has slides along the luff and a sewn-in cord for the foot. Discuss with the sail maker the amount of chamber appropriate for your anticipated type of sailing and the wind and sea conditions under which you are likely to sail. These factors will also decide the need for reef points, if any.

Telltales are essential for determining the correct angle of sail to the wind, steering, and proper sail trim. They are indispensible for knowing how the wind flows across the sail surface, which parts of the sail are pulling their weight and which are stalling. But don't have too many telltales, there is a limit to the amount of information the skipper and crew can digest and use effectively. The mainsail needs telltales only on the leech streaming out from the batten pockets. The front sail needs telltales both in the leech and some pairs, one for each side, just in from the luff. In light and medium winds telltales mostly help steering when close-hauled and determining sail trim when reaching. In heavy winds ignore telltales. A good sail maker will discuss and offer advice on the best number and location of telltales. Sailing texts discuss the behaviour of telltales and their significance but a few general remarks appear below.

Finally, sails need to be cleaned, dried, and properly stored in a dry place during the off-season. Flaking sails is to fold sails in an accordion pleat 600 mm to 100 mm in width. To flake a sail properly, start at the foot and keep the pleat square to the luff for the mail sail. For the front sail start at the foot and keep the pleat square to the leech. Then roll the pleat from clew to tack into a neat, manageable package.

## Trailer

The Dragon's weight and full, deep keel requires a custom-built, two-axle trailer. Basically the flat of the keel rests on a center beam low to the ground and the hull is kept in balance by four support points. Ensure that there is about 400 lbs. weight on the tongue to prevent undue sway while it is pulled. In the absence of a hoist the boat may need to be launched from a ramp, as is the case with *Lady Jayne*. That requires a few more considerations. While going down the ramp and the boat levels to the water, the bow lowers relative to the trailer. To prevent undue pressure on the front supports, it is best to remove or lower those supports before proceeding down the ramp. Also, allowing the hull to pivot at the point where the keel rests on the trailer lessens the depth of water required to float the hull off the trailer. Even at that, the depth needed is considerable and will require an extension to the trailer tongue. Alternatively, disconnect the trailer from the vehicle and use a chain between the vehicle and the trailer to let the trailer find appropriate depth to float off the hull and then to retrieve the trailer.

Collapsible support to ease hull off trailer

*Lady Jayne's* trailer has one collapsible support combining the two front support points. It folds down for the launch and retrieval of the boat. Also, the winch is mounted on a particularly tall post to bring it well above deck level. The winch cable attaches to a chain temporarily looped around the mast pulpit. That distance between the winch and the mast pulpit is crucial for allowing the bow sufficient up and down movement.

As an added benefit, there is no need for a stainless steel bow-eye to disgrace the strikingly beautiful wooden bow.

Mounting the winch high up also facilitates the winch's second function – lifting the mast. Lifting the mast requires a medium to heavy-duty winch. When preparing to take the boat in and out of the water, align the bow with the winch support post but protect the sharply pointed bow with a sturdy wood covering. On the trailer affix some supports on either side of the keel to funnel it and the hull into its precise place on the trailer when taking the boat out of the water. During the off-season *Lady Jayne* is stored in the boat house on the trailer. To preserve the suspension system and ease the tires the trailer's frame rests on blocks for the duration.

## Erecting Mast

The mast is stored along one wall of the boathouse about one metre up from the floor resting on support brackets. During transport, the mast is flat on the hull resting on the mast pulpit and an especially built support leg near the transom. Using two sets of blocks lift the mast horizontally from the supports that line the boat house wall. Lift it to just above deck height, then ease it sideways over the deck and position mast suitable for transport.

Before launching the boat, raise the mast. Start by tensioning the strut wires with a Loos model B tension meter to about 20. Align the mast's Oak dowels with their matching notches at the top of the mast pulpit.

A temporary support is clamped to the forward side of the pulpit. This support, constructed with two, 38 mm by 89 mm, is nearly 2 meters tall with a sheave at the top and just as wide as the pulpit. Lay the forestay over the sheave and attach the forestay to the trailer winch cable. This temporary support creates enough height to lift the mast. When constructing the support affix a few blocks on the aft side, just above the Oak dowels. It will prevent the mast from jumping the pulpit during the first segment of lifting. As the mast rises its own weight will prevent any tendency to jump.

While raising the mast with the winch, the trailer must be level from side to side, lest the mast sway sideways. Before the mast is completely up, stuff the halyards from inside the mast down the pulpit to be retrieved below deck. Temporarily hold the mast up with some rope. Release the forestay from the winch and bring it down alongside the mast; then mark the top of the Black Band with tape or marker. Next, loosely attach the forestay and the shrouds to their attachments inside the hull. The mast is secure from toppling and fine-tuning can begin.

Temporary support to give lift to mast

Mast rake can now be determined. Tighten the forestay till the distance from the Black Band mark to the deck measured along the forestay is 120 cm for light winds and 122 cm for heavy winds.

Now comes a moment of truth verifying your skills at the lofting and hull construction done years before. If the forestay attachment and the mast pulpit are both in their correct location the distances should be as follows: 82 cm from mast to Station Four and 104 cm from Station Four to the forestay measured along the Centre Line at deck level.

It is a mite humbling to admit but when I reached this point in *Lady Jayne* I was glad the forestay attachment at the keelsom is adjustable.

Mast rake is always critical but particularly in the Dragon. Mast rake determines the amount of weather helm and pointing ability. Weather helm refers to the tendency of the hull to come up-wind when sailing close-hauled. Lee helm is the opposite. Some weather helm is to be expected but only a little. Too much is a drag on performance. Rudder needs to be applied to counter weather helm, which is like a brake, preventing the hull from running free. A well-balanced hull requires no rudder pressure when close-hauled in light to medium winds and only moderate pressure in heavy winds. In nearly all weather conditions and points of sail the tiller should require no more than two or three fingertips for steering. Many boats suffer from too much weather helm to the point of skippers bracing themselves and heaving with all their might to prevent the bow turning windward, a sure sign of a badly balanced hull.

Usually reducing rake will reduce weather helm. In addition, rake also affects pointing ability. In most cases reducing rake improves pointing ability. Hence, it is counter-productive to have more rake than needed. However, reducing rake more than needed affects speed negatively. Experimentation is appropriate but in very small measures.[38]

Next tension the shrouds. Using the Loos tension meter put 20 on the Upper shrouds. That is for shrouds without plastic covering. Assuming that the shrouds for port and starboard are exactly the same length, an equal distance from the deck to the end of the shroud for both sides will ensure the mast is perpendicular to the hull. Tension the Lower shrouds at 5 and look along the sail channel on the mast's aft side to ensure it is perfectly straight. In heavy winds tension on the Lower shrouds should be lessened even more to allow the mast to drop off leeward narrowing the gap and making the rig less powerful.

The forestay's tension is determined by the running backstays. Tension one of the backstays until the forestay reads 30 on the meter. Mark the running backstay with tape at the point it enters the deck. Repeat for the other backstay. When a backstay is pulled just tight the distance between the tape mark and the deck should be 150 mm. In light wind (i.e. up to 6 knots) the running backstays are pulled just tight showing 150 mm of wire from deck to the tape mark. In heavy winds (i.e. more than 17 knots) the tape mark is brought to the deck. For medium winds place the mark halfway.

The backstay is adjusted during sailing depending on wind conditions. In light winds it needs very little tension and may be used to keep the top batten parallel with the boom. In heavy wind apply sufficient

---

38    Weather helm and pointing ability result from many factors, not just rake, and are discussed at length in most sailing texts. A good internet source is at: http://johnellsworth.com/writing/nautical/balance_helm/balance.html

tension to bend the mast thereby flattening the sail and also to open the mainsail's leech. When running before the wind release the backstay to maximize the sail area exposed to the wind regardless of wind strength.

Set to raise mast

## Sailing the Dragon

The Dragon is a high performance boat mostly used for racing with a three-person crew. It has remained at the top level of competitive sailing over the years and shows no sign of diminished interest among high-performance competitors, world-wide. But the Dragon is versatile. It can be sailed single-handedly with ease and great pleasure for simple day sailings. Hence, after all these years it is still among the world's most popular one-design classes. The Dragon's secret is largely a wonderfully balanced sail plan that makes boat handling easy even for skippers of slight build and light weight. Unlike some other sail boat classes, great performance in the Dragon does not require maximum crew weight and top fitness.

The Dragon's performance is attained solely through sailing skills, hence its attraction to persons of all age groups and skill levels.

This book is not about sailing technique and strategy as there are many specialized texts for that purpose, but a few basic principles are included here for the sake of completeness. Also some of these sailing tips may be peculiar to the Dragon, or less well-known, such as handling running backstays. My recommendations for sailing *Lady Jayne* include the following:

*Changing tack when close-hauled*, the appropriate sequence after the skipper's command to "come about";
1. turn tiller;
2. release front sail sheet;
3. bring up the 'off duty' running backstay;
4. release the 'working' running backstay;
5. bring up the front sail sheet.

In light winds these can be done leisurely, in heavy winds they must be performed flawlessly and in quick succession.

*Changing tack from close-hauled to downwind,* wing-on-wing sequence:
1. Decide which side to have boom and wheth-er to jibe or bring bow through wind;
2. Inform crew and assign tasks;
3. Turn tiller;
4. Bring up "off duty" running backstay;
5. Release:
   a. Out haul;
   b. Cunningham;
   c. Main sheet;
   d. "On-duty" backstay.
6. Bring boom out against shroud;
7. Attach and set boom restrainer;
8. Set main sheet;
9. Clip on life-line;
10. Insert whisker pole into genoa clew and attach to mast;

11. Set front sail sheet.

*If over-powered or too much weather helm:*
1. Flatten main sail in this sequence:
   a. Increase tension on halyard;
   b. Increase tension on Cunningham;
   c. Increase tension on outhaul (1-3 might require bearing off and/or releasing mainsheet);
   d. Increase tension on backstay to yield more mast bend;
   e. Increase tension on boom vang;
   f. Increase tension on main sheet;
   g. Bring traveller windward.
2. Put more twist in genoa leech (freeing the leech);
3. Move the traveller leeward;
4. If needed to prevent leech flutter tension the main sail leech cord;
5. Ease off the mainsheet thereby twisting or freeing the leech and generating some backwind on the luff;
6. Move weight aft.

Solo sailing at Pender Harbour

## Main sail settings close-hauled

In light wind and smooth seas adjust the halyard, Cunningham, and outhaul to keep the sail full. The traveller is moved slightly windward but the boom is kept just below the center line and the boom vang is completely slack. In choppy conditions the sail should be less full, lest the wind stalls along the sail's outside surface.

In medium wind apply more tension on the sheet, the backstay, running backstay, and the boom vang. The traveller is moved on the center line or beyond if the wind increases, use the outhaul to bring the clew to the Black Band. Keep experimenting to attain best trim.

In heavy wind bring the sail in and flatten the sail. If less power is needed move the traveller further below center line. As the wind increases flatten the sails more and more with all the adjustments listed above with particular attention to increased mast bend.

## Genoa settings close-hauled

In light winds and smooth seas the halyard is almost slack leaving horizontal lines in the luff. The tension on foot and leech is almost equal and the leech cord slack. Bring genoa close to spreaders and shrouds. In choppy seas ease genoa away from spreader and shroud. Also put some tension on the running backstay.

In medium winds increase the luff tension almost removing the horizontal creases. The gap between genoa and main should be narrowed for better pointing but just shy of luffing the main. In choppy seas widen the gap slightly for more power. Running backstay tension should be increased as winds build.

In heavy winds the halyard tension needs to be at maximum to help pointing ability and all horizontal creases are removed. In extreme conditions luffing of main may be necessary to keep hull upright and genoa leech needs to be freed.

## Telling Tales

Steering upwind can be greatly aided by telltales sewn into the genoa near the luff. Fluttering of leeward telltales indicates sailing too low and fluttering of windward telltales indicates pointing too high. Hence, to make the appropriate corrections remember: *"Tiller Towards Fluttering Telltale."*

These steering telltales in the genoa indicate maximum performance of sail trim, angle to wind, and sideways drift. But the behaviour of the telltales depends on wind strength. In light winds, telltales on both sides should stream aft with the windward telltales about to jump and twirl. In medium winds, the windward telltales need to jump at steady intervals. In heavy winds the importance of telltales diminishes.

## Right-of-way Rules

Right-of-way rules for sailboats, particularly racing rules, are many and complex. Official publications should be consulted for complete information. The following are the most general rules expressed in everyday, non-legal language.

1. A boat on *starboard tack* has right-of-way over a boat on *port tack*. Generally, this rule can be expressed as: *If you are sitting on the right, you are in the right,* (provided your boom is out on the opposite side of where you sit).
2. A *leeward boat* has right-of-way over a *windward boat*. (A windward boat is nearer, or closer to the wind than a leeward boat)
3. A boat *clear ahead* has right-of-way over a boat *clear astern*.
4. A windward boat, if establishing an overlap from clear astern of a leeward boat, if need be, shall sail head to wind to keep clear.
5. A *boat on a tack* has right-of-way over a boat that alters course by *tacking or jibing*.
6. A *right-of-way boat*, when altering course, must allow room for a *burdened boat* to stay clear. (A burdened boat is the 'give-way' boat, the boat that does not have the right-of-way)

7. At marks or obstructions an *outside boat* shall not prevent an *inside boat* from rounding the mark or clearing the obstruction.

These brief suggestions cover some general instructions about sailing but each hull and local sea condition requires its own peculiar response and the right-of-way rules are the most general expressed in non-technical language.

Sailing is an art never fully mastered. The most experienced sailors readily admit that learning never stops. It is what makes sailing endlessly fascinating, challenging, and satisfying. Above all, sailing is about taking delight in the journey.

*Lady Jayne* participating in the Garden Bay Sailing Club's weekly race

# APPENDIX (SAW FILING)

## Cross-cut Saws[39], How it is Done

To sharpen a saw, place it in a vise, teeth up. A triangular file is placed in a gullet and pushed away from you. On each stroke downward pressure is applied to remove some steel. When the file is brought back it is lifted slightly to not touch the steel.

The file is held at an angle relative to the length of the saw. The direction of the angle is such that the file's tip always points toward the saw's tip. In other words, the file is pushed away from the saw's handle.

Teeth are alternately bend one way and the other way. Hence, half the teeth are filed from one side of the saw, the saw is then turned end-for-end and the remaining teeth are filed from the other side of the saw.

On each side, starting from the handle, the file is pushed through every alternate gullet. Starting from the handle the first gullet to be filed has the bend-away tooth between the file and the saw handle. *This latter point is very important!*

A needle sharp saw requires that the file be kept at precise angles relative to the saw. These angles much be maintained for each stroke through each gullet on each side. There three such angles.

---

39     Useful reference is found in: Disston Saw, Tool and File Manual, *How to Sharpen a Hand Saw*, Henry Disston & Sons, Inc, Philadelphia, PA, 1952

**Angle One** is the easiest. The file should be held level. Do not file uphill or downhill. Hence, the angle is ninety degrees between the file and the saw's side. Usually that means keeping the file parallel to the floor.

**Angle Two** is the angle at which the file crosses the length of the saw. This angle is a little more difficult to keep steady from gullet to gullet and from one side to the next. It helps to have a small jig, or block of wood that is cut with the appropriate angle. This little jig slides along atop the teeth close to the file. It provides a constant guide.

**Angle Three** is the tilt of the file across its beam (since this is all about boats). The file is held such that one of the flat sides of the file is on top. But this flat side is not horizontal. It is a little off, it is tilted. This angle is the most difficult to maintain. It is affected by any twisting of the wrist. Again a small jig is the answer. This jig is fastened to the tip of the file. Keeping the jig horizontal ensures the file tilt is correct.

**What is Needed**

You will need a number of cross-cut hand saws from a regular eight teeth per 25 mm to a very fine tooth, stiff-backed saw. Sharpening cross-cut hand saws requires the following:
- an assortment of tapered triangular files
- one flat, mill bastard file
- a fine-tooth setting tool
- a coarse-tooth setting tool
- a vise and good lighting
  Personally, for very fine-toothed saws I also need a magnifying lamp.
  File sizes appropriate to teeth sizes are in a table printed on the package in which files are sold. When buying files, don't buy junk! It is a waste of time and money. They will not cut the steel. Buy high quality only, such as the Sandvik or Nicholson brands. Discard dull files. Files that screech at you are beyond their 'best before date'. Throw them out.

Before a file can be used it must be fitted with a handle, easily made from hardwood or a length of dried Douglas Fir, or any fruit tree branch.

To hold the saw firmly in place I use an old fashioned, wooden saw-sharpening vise, or horse (fig. 6). The correct height is six inches below your armpit. The advantage of a wooden vise over a steel bench vise is its height, allowing you to stand up instead of bending over. And it also allows sharpening a whole side at once. The top of the rails on the vise part should have a 45 degree bevel.

FIG. #6   OLD FASHIONED SAW SHARPENING
HORSE FOR FILING HAND SAWS

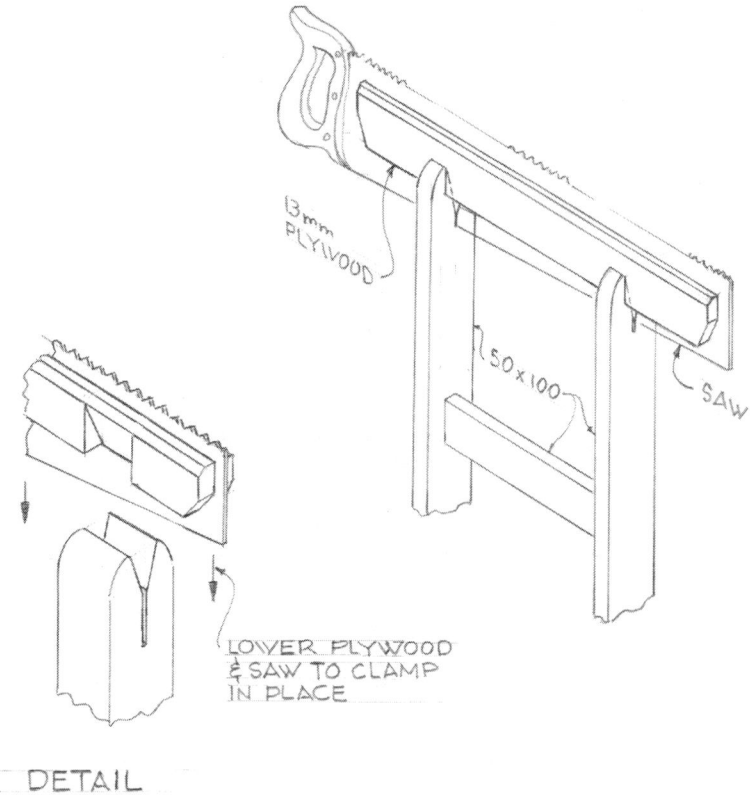

13 mm PLYWOOD

50 x 100

SAW

LOWER PLYWOOD & SAW TO CLAMP IN PLACE

DETAIL

Make jigs or guiding blocks as follows. For cross-cut saws the bevel angle (Angle Two), is twenty-five degrees.

Use a small block of hardwood about 25 mm long, 18 mm wide and 18 mm inch thick. Saw a slot 6 mm deep at twenty-five degrees in the centre of one of the 18 mm wide surfaces. Do the same from the opposing surface such that the two slots are parallel, on top of each other, they should not cross each other.

Next, make a rake jig (Angle Three). For a cross-cut saw, rake should be fifteen degrees off straight up and down. Make a jig 37 mm long, 25 mm wide, 12 mm thick out of hardwood to fit on the tip of the file. In the centre of one of the 12 mm sides drill a hole of such a size that when the file is inserted and tapped into place it will fit snug and stay in place. Drill all the way through the jig.

Mark one of the flat sides as 'top' and add an arrow pointing to the right side of this surface and mark that arrow 'handle'. Then, using a protractor, mark a line on the side facing you, just to the right of the hole. The line should be fifteen degrees off straight up and down and angle from the surface marked 'top' down *towards the left*. Turn the jig end for end. The arrow will now point left. On this side mark a similar line, but now on the left side of the hole, sloping *towards the right*. The rake jig is now complete. Insert the tip of the file into the hole you drilled on the side of your jig. Insert the file such that one side of the file is parallel to the angled line. Then gentle tap the file in place with a mallet. Remove it and do the same for the other side. You now have a rake jig. You are ready to start but first place the saw correctly in the vise.

For placing the saw in the vise, the two, top rails of the sharpening vise are lifted, the saw placed between them with just the teeth showing plus a bit, then wedged in place and tapped snug with a rubber mallet. The saw must be held firmly.

Jig on saw and jig on file to maintain correct angles

Vibration makes the file skip and fails to produce a sharp cutting edge on the tooth. If needed, place two c-clamps on the rails between the upright supports. It will prevent any movement in the saw blade while filing.

Next, the flat mill file is pushed across the teeth along the length of the saw to file down the high points, making all teeth level in height. The teeth will have a small flat spot, some more than others. If there is considerable unevenness in the size and height of teeth it will show in some teeth having much larger flat areas than others and some gullets will be much deeper than others. In addition, the rake may not be even on all teeth. If any of these conditions hold take some time to shape the teeth. Make flat areas, gullets and rake the same for all teeth. This is how it is done.

When filing pay close attention to the various angles at which the file is held. At first, it may all seem a bit much. However, after doing a dozen teeth it comes naturally, and before long you'll do it without thinking. Select those teeth that need shaping, find the appropriate gullet, place the tapered tip of the file into the gullet, line up the file parallel to the little jig that is resting on the saw, see that the rake jig on the end of your file parallels the saw, and that the file is horizontal along its length. In that exact position, push the full length of the file through the gullet. If necessary, repeat till one half of the flat area is removed. The other half will be removed when you shape teeth from the other side of the saw.

Every over-sized tooth has an under-sized neighbour. Suppressing the mighty and exalting the lowly (I write just before Christmas) requires significant sideways pressure and keen eyesight. Start with the worst offenders. Even doing just those improves cutting performance significantly.

When equality is restored on this side, turn the saw end-for-end to shape the other side. Remove the rake jig and insert the file from the opposite edge, keep the top up and the arrow pointed to the saw's handle. The bevel angle jig that rides on top of the teeth is turned over. After all teeth have the same size and shape, they need to be re-set.

Teeth are set simply by squeezing the setting tool against each tooth that is bent away from you, first the teeth on one side then the other[40]. The set determines the width of the cut or kerf. Setting tools are adjustable to increase or decrease the width of the cut. The correct width depends on the stock to be cut. Soft lumber, particularly with high moisture content, requires maximum set for a wide kerf. Kiln and dried hardwood requires a minimal set for a narrow kerf.

After the shaping and setting comes the final filing. Once more, run the mill file along the teeth to give each a small flat top. Then, check off this list.

- The file is angled such that the pointed end of the file is away from the saw handle and the file is parallel to the bevel angle jig.
- The file rests in the first gullet near the handle such that the bent-away tooth is between the file and the handle.
- The rake jig's surface is parallel to the top of the teeth.
- The file is level, parallel to the floor.

---

40    Some set the saw after filing. I was taught to do it first and have always followed this practice.

You file the first appropriate gullet and every second one after that. Each stroke files the front and therefore the cutting edge of the tooth that is bent away from you and the same stroke files the back of the tooth bent towards you. You need more pressure toward the left because that tooth, the one bent towards you, will tend to vibrate slightly, making the file less efficient in removing steel. Failure to compensate results in smaller teeth on one side than those on the other side. On each side remove half of the flat area. You may not need more than two or three strokes through each gullet. The bevelled cutting edges should be keen all the way down the gullet.

The secret to expert filing is not only a steady hand but also good eyesight assisted by strong lighting. Keen observation of tooth size and gullet depth is important. To produce an even tooth-size pattern, the filer must adjust the sideway pressure as the file passes between the teeth. This takes practice and experience.

Lastly, when the filing is done, lay the saw on the workbench with the teeth over the edge. Take a sturdy rag with oil and vigorously rub from the blade out across the teeth. This will remove filing bits, flatten the tiny burr on the tooth edge, and oil the blade to prevent rust. It is impossible to file a keen cutting edge on a saw blade pitted by rust. Don't allow rust to develop; always keep the blade shiny by oiling it.

Congratulations! Your saw is needle-sharp and it will cut clean and straight. You have mastered an art. The art is not difficult but since it requires much patience, few practise it.

# GLOSSARY

| | |
|---|---|
| *bilge* | lowest part of the hull where water collects and from there pumped out. |
| *block* | a pulley, or system of pulleys mounted in a case. |
| *brightwork* | wood finished with a clear, transparent finish to show the grain. |
| *close-hauled* | sailing as close towards the direction of the wind as possible. |
| *gusset* | a piece of wood to reinforce the joint where the ribs meet to form a frame when joined together. |
| *headstock mandrel* | part of a lathe which is nearest the source of power and grips one end of the stock. |
| *keelsom* | the main beam that runs from stem to stern at the Centre Line where ribs meet at the lowest point inside the hull. |
| *mast pulpit* | the stand that supports the mast at deck level. |
| *port* | the left-hand side of a hull when facing forward. |

| | |
|---|---|
| *rabbet* | a groove or step cut along the length of a piece of wood usually to be joined by another piece of wood. |
| *rake* | the angle at which the mast leans aft, also the angle of the teeth of a hand saw. |

### sail parts

| | |
|---|---|
| *luff* | leading edge |
| *leech* | trailing edge |
| *foot* | bottom edge |
| *head* | point where luff and leech meet |
| *tack* | point where luff and foot meet |
| *clew* | point where leech and foot meet |
| *sheave* | the wheel with a grooved rim inside a block. |
| *sheer* | the line where hull and deck meet. |
| *sheet* | rope to control the setting of a sail. |
| *sole* | the floor of the cockpit. |
| *spline* | a thin piece of wood that fits into the edge or end of a piece of wood to prevent it splitting or to join two larger pieces of wood. |
| *starboard* | the right-hand side of a hull when facing forward. |
| *stuffing box* | an enclosure that contains packing to prevent leakage around the propeller shaft usually located where the shaft penetrates the hull. |
| *tack* | change in direction while sailing. |

| | |
|---|---|
| *tail head* | part of a lathe furthest away from the source of power and grips one end of the stock. |
| *whisker pole* | light pole for extending the clew of the front sail, used in place of a spinnaker pole. |

## About the Author

Nick Loenen grew up in Nieuw Loosdrecht, the Netherlands, a water wonderland, particularly for sailing. As a teenager he immigrated with his family to Vancouver, where he lives with his wife Jayne. While pursuing a business career in residential construction he sailed his Flying Dutchman on Vancouver's English Bay. Since retirement he sails the much admired Lady Jayne around the Pender Harbour area of British Columbia's strikingly beautiful coast and indulges his passion for wood working.

## About the Illustrator

Hans Bomhof was born in Rotterdam, immigrated to Victoria, Canada as a child and has lived most of his adult life in Vancouver. He has owned several boats and has enjoyed sailing the coast of British Columbia and Washington State. He spent several years in Indonesia as Senior Mechanical Designer of Pulp Mills and Power Plants with SNC Lavalin. Now retired, Hans and his wife Lainie enjoy spending time, whenever they can, at their lake-side house they designed and built.